Jewish Latin America

Jewish Latin America
Ilan Stavans, series editor

THE JEWISH GAUCHOS OF THE PAMPAS

the JEWISH GAUCHOS

of the Pampas

ALBERTO GERCHUNOFF

Translated by
PRUDENCIO DE PEREDA

Foreword by
ILAN STAVANS

University of New Mexico Press
Albuquerque

Library of Congress Cataloging-in-Publication Data

Gerchunoff, Alberto, 1883–1950.
   [Gauchos judíos. English]
   Jewish gauchos of the pampas / Alberto Gerchunoff ; translated by Prudencio de Pereda ; foreword by Ilan Stavans.
      p.   cm. — (Jewish Latin America)
   ISBN 0-8263-1767-7
   1. Jews—Argentina—Entre Ríos—Fiction.   2. Gauchos—Argentina—Entre Ríos—Fiction.   I. Pereda, Prudencio de.   II. Title.
III. Series.
PQ7797.G4G313   1998
863—dc21   97-38279
                                                        CIP

The Jewish Gauchos of the Pampas *is the first volume in the University of New Mexico Press series* Jewish Latin America. *Wood engravings by Victor L. Reboffo. Minor changes have been made to the original English translation. The editor is grateful to Jacobo Kovadloff, Marjorie Agosín, Stephen A. Sadow, and Naomi Lindstrom for their help in the preparation of this book.*

To the revered memory of Baron Moisés de Hirsch,
founder of the Jewish colonies in the Argentine Republic.
His was the first bread that my people ate on American soil,
and with the homage of simple gratitude, I place his
name at the front of this book.

contents

foreword
ILAN STAVANS

L'art est un anti-destin.

ANDRÉ MALRAUX

Up until very recently, the Spanish language resisted embracing the Jewish sensibility. This becomes clear in a sentence found in the 1974 edition of the *Encyclopædia Judaica*, in which *The Jewish Gauchos of the Pampas* is described as "the first work of literary value to be written in Spanish by a Jew in modern times." The astonishing implication is that roughly between 1492 and 1910, when Alberto Gerchunoff, a Russian émigré to Argentina, compiled his twenty-six interrelated fictional vignettes on life in Moisésville and Rajíl, agri-cultural communities sponsored by Baron Maurice de Hirsch in South America in the late nineteenth century into a hymn to tran-sculturation in the Pampas, not a single literary item of merit ap-peared in the language. Prior to their expulsion from the Iberian peninsula, Jews prayed in Hebrew and wrote in Aramaic and Latin, but communicated mostly in Ladino (i.e., *Spanioli* or Judeo-Spanish), a hybrid blend of Castilian, Hebrew, Turkish, Arabic, and other verbal elements. Which means that the only literature by Jews in Spanish before *The Jewish Gauchos* is a product of *marranos*, crypto-Jews, and new Christians and, by definition, it falsifies and misrepresents, it denies its Jewishness.

No wonder Gerchunoff is such a quixotic figure: his lifelong project, to turn Spanish into a home for the Jews, to acclimate the language not only to Hebraisms and Yiddishisms but to a *weltanschauung* totally alien to it, went against the currents of history. In fact, he was not only a modern literateur, as the *Encyclopædia Judaica* describes him but, more important, part of the *modernista* generation that renewed Hispanic American letters between 1885 and 1915. It did it by drawing heavily upon Parnassianism and Symbolism and by establishing a new crystalline and harmonious Spanish syntax based on restraint and precision, a new language musically elegant and spiritedly metaphorical. Gerchunoff befriended Rubén Darío, Leopoldo Lugones, and Delmira Agustini—a Nicaraguan, an Argentine, and an Uruguayan respectively, all four pillars of the *modernista* literary revolution. But his struggle went beyond: born into Yiddish, he appropriated Quevedo's tongue, making it his own, and dreamed of inserting Spanish-speaking Jews into the twentieth century by building a three-way bridge among Renaissance Spain, nineteenth-century Russia and Eastern Europe, and modern Hispanic America. An authentic polyglot (aside from Yiddish and Spanish, he was fluent in Italian, French, English, Portuguese, and Russian), his heroes were Spinoza and Heinrich Heine, both uprooted speakers and "alien guests," as well as Sholem Aleichem and Cervantes, whose verbal talent and florid imagination explain the two facades of Gerchunoff: his Jewish side and his Hispanic side. Not surprisingly, Miguel de Unamuno once described him as "the cosmopolitan man of letters *sine qua non*."

His enterprise wasn't easy, though. It often clashed against insurmountable obstacles within and without his milieu: scattered outbursts of anti-Semitism and an occasional pogrom in Argentina, and the extermination of his direct ancestry in Europe. His views on socialism and democracy, on freedom and Jewish morality often pushed him against his people, turning him into an outcast. In his twenties, for instance, Gerchunoff portrayed Argentina as a *país de advenimiento,* a Promised Land, the real Palestine where Jews could thrive in total harmony with gentiles. But his hope quickly tuned sour in 1919 with the *semana trágica,* an explosion of xenophobia that amounted to a full-blown pogrom in Buenos Aires. By then he had already been a member of the Partido Socialista and had switched to the Partido Demócrata Progresista, had been incarcerated for a brief period for siding with Cuba during the Spanish-American War, had fought against the right-wing "radicalism" of President Hipólito Irigoyen, and, after a visit to Germany, had actively campaigned against its anti-Jewish sentiments. All this pushed Gerchunoff inwards: he became more introspective and mystical, less hopeful of earthly utopias. He was often accused of being too slow to recognize and publicly denounce the existence of anti-Semitism. His strategy was to put the best face on Jewish-gentile relations, and this relentlessly positive outlook cut down on his ability to criticize evil tendencies in society. Still, he never lost his militant edge: a couple of decades later, in an unpopular stand at home, he was active gathering support against Hitler and became the most prominent Hispanic American intellectual to tackle "the Jewish problem"—that is, the homelessness of the Jewish people in the diaspora. Then, between 1945 and his death, already suffering from a heart condition, he traveled within Argentina and beyond—to Brazil, Chile, and Peru—to harvest political support for Zionism. Eliezer ben Yehudah had metamorphosed Hebrew into *the* Promised Land, but Gerchunoff was already too old to master it. The *zeitgeist* of history had taken him to the wrong Palestine, and he was forced to recognize Spanish as another diasporic home for the Jewish people, not the center stage he had believed it to be.

In this foreword I'm considerably less interested in his end than in his beginnings. According to his passport, Gerchunoff was born in Proskuroff, Russia, on January 1, 1883; his mother dissented though (and scholars concur): it was in 1884, she claimed, "and into the Yiddish language." Yiddish, indeed, was in the milk he drank and in the early Talmudic lessons he got, to the point that, when he switched to Spanish around 1894, thanks to a Sephardic teacher, Don Moisés Urquijo de Abenoim, traces of his Yiddish background could be found, as Gerchunoff himself says in an article compiled in his posthumous collection *The Pine and the Palm Tree*, "in the verbal choices and sentence structures I made." He remained loyal to his mother tongue until his death, using it in his mature age to deliver speeches and lectures at the Sociedad Hebráica in Buenos Aires, a distinguished Jewish-community association he helped found. Actually, one might be able to go as far as to say that *The Jewish Gauchos* was thought out in Yiddish, yet written in Spanish. Its pages have a unique syntax, in part owing to Gerchunoff's purist *modernista* approach, for which he became widely known as editorialist, and in part to his Yiddish ascendancy; and they are seasoned with transliterations from the Hebrew pronounced with a heavy Yiddish accent. This magnificent act of tongue-switching highlights Gerchunoff's need to belong. The characters in his book, stationed as they are in a southern agricultural milieu, are natural descendants of Mendele Mokher Sforim, Sholem Aleichem, and Isaac Leib Peretz. The narrator admits this via such indications as "the woman answered *en judío*—in Jewish." And yet he favors Sephardic references over Eastern European ones. Gerchunoff probably considered Yiddish not lofty and august enough to embrace it as his literary vehicle, yet he keeps it alive in his reader's unconscious by modifying his stylized Spanish to invoke its rhythm and cadence. Isn't this further proof that the written word always means more than it says?

Proskuroff was a small shtetl and, as such, it was inhabited solely by lower-class Jews with a modicum of self-sufficiency. In 1886 the Gerchunoffs moved to Tulchin, where "In the Beginning," the opening chapter of *The Jewish Gauchos*, takes place. It was a "sordid and sad" city, he wrote, where the family stayed several months. Cossacks were attacking, "crushing the old walls of the synagogues and the ancient sanctuaries on whose pinnacle the double triangle of Solomon stood shining," and burning "the sacred books of the city's leading synagogue," when Baron de Hirsch, thinking that Zion could well be established in Argentina, appeared in the collective imagination of Tulchin as a messiah. They began hearing about de Hirsch's Jewish Colonization Association, and an envoy was sent to Paris to discuss possible resettlements. He returned with happy news: "Baron de Hirsch—may God bless him!—has promised to save us." With his help the Gerchunoffs traveled first to Berlin and then to Dresden; later on they took the ship *Pampa*, crossing the Atlantic; finally, after a month-long stay at the *Hotel de Inmigrantes*, a transit post in Buenos Aires, they arrived in Moisésville, an agricultural colony in the Santa Fé province (named after Baron de Hirsch's deceased son, Moisés), chanting:

> To Palestine, to the Argentine,
> We'll go—to sow;
> To live as friends and brothers;
> To be free!

Latin America enjoyed relative stability during the last quarter of the nineteenth century. Eager to open its provinces to entrepreneurial settlers to populate the immense, labor-scarce nation, Argentina, up until World War I, attracted a huge number of immigrants, some from the Ottoman Empire but most of them from Eastern Europe and Russia. (From the latter 158,167 Jews alone entered between 1889 and 1914.) Many settled in the provinces of Santa Fé and Entre Ríos, touching off the greatest social change on the Pampa. Argentine statesmen favored the European newcomers, often called *gringos* by the gauchos. Juan Bautista Alberdi, for instance, was responsible for the famous dictum: "To govern is to populate." Domingo Faustino Sarmiento, author of the classic *Civilization and Barbarism: Life of Don Facundo Quiroga,* saw them as an influx of "civilized" life in a vastly barbaric landscape. Gringos and gauchos seldom competed directly for employment because the former were farmers and the latter herdsmen.

The definitive social origin of the gaucho in the Southern Hemisphere still lies shrouded in ambiguity: some emphasize his Andalusian and Arabic roots; others call attention to his *mestizo* heritage—a racial and cultural blending of Indian and Iberian components—and believe the term *gaucho* comes either from the Guarani *huach* or *huachú,* or from the Quechua *huak-cha.* What is unquestionable is that, since the gaucho's appearance around 1745, his costumes and habits changed substantially, always at a slower speed than the negative sentiments against him, which ultimately improved around 1872, when José Hernández published his poetic defense, *The Gaucho Martín Fierro,* now held as a national treasure. Before then, the gaucho was approached as a "pastoral" person, "ignorant and cruel," "oppressed" and "in an incipient stage of civilization," an antipathy resulting from the clash between urban and rural populations. But Hernández's revolution came too late; as a result of a juggernaut of changes forcing him to abandon his tradition, the gaucho ceased to exist as an identifiable social type during the last third of the nineteenth century. Coincidentally, his last sights coincided with Gerchunoff's arrival in Moisésville.

This coincidence is symptomatic. All in all, Gerchunoff spent a total of five years as a *gaucho judío,* from the ages of six to eleven. In Moisésville he began attending school, where he learned mathematics, Argentine history and geography, and the rules and grammar of Spanish. In 1891 a tragic event, which appears in the section "The

Death of Reb Saul" of *The Jewish Gauchos,* made them tremble: his father, a businessman and Talmudist who "spoke very little Spanish but he spoke energetically," was killed by a vengeful gaucho. Profoundly saddened, Gerchunoff's mother decided to move the family to Rajíl, another agricultural settlement where the future writer "learned the stanzas of the national anthem." In 1895, they all settled in Buenos Aires, where Gerchunoff got his first job in a matzoh bakery.

Moisésville and Rajíl were small and somewhat isolated, but they were not shtetls in the strict sense of the word: Jews didn't inhabit an isolated island; natives lived in near proximity, constantly interacting with them to the point of transculturation. In the chapter "The Poet," for example, Favel Duglach, a lazy but well-regarded colonist with an artistic twist, "could feel the native Argentine epics of bravery with the same exaltation he experienced when telling some story from the Bible to a tense, expectant group in the synagogue." Gerchunoff describes Duglach as

> an original-looking man. A hooked nose dominated his face, and his long beard was balanced by long locks of hair at the back of his head. He wore the loose gaucho trousers, the *bombachas,* under his traditional Jewish cassock, that was belted in his case. It was a fantastic getup, but Favel explained the absurdities by stating: "I'm a Jewish Gaucho."

Other similar intercourses abound: in the Entre Ríos of Gerchunoff, Jews attend *cuadreras* (i.e., rodeos), listen to gaucho stories with biblical undertones around the warming *fogata,* and fall in love with gentile *boyeros* while singing beautifully sad songs, known as *vidalitas.* They both admire the gaucho and fear him, conceiving "his life as a thrilling amalgam of heroism and barbarism," and wanting to be like him—but with reservations; they also perceive themselves as Jews and their success in the new land depends on the balancing of an ancestral tradition and the exposure to a form of cowboy life previously unknown to them.

The term *gaucho judío* was called an oxymoron by Jorge Luis Borges. "[*The Jewish Gauchos*] is less a truthful historical document than a testimonial of nostalgia," he argued. He published several important essays and edited several anthologies on the gaucho in Argentine culture. In a lecture delivered at the Colegio Libre de Estudios Superiores in Buenos Aires (*Discusión*, 2nd ed., 1955), he established the difference between *poesía de los gauchos* and *poesía gauchesca*: the first is a gathering of popular voices of the Pampas, whereas the second is made of the "artificial" works of urban writers interested in the gaucho. By definition, the *guachesco* writers pervert and falsify—and although Borges never acknowledges Gerchunoff by name (his immense admiration for his Jewish friend precluded any attacks), his portrayal of the Jewish gaucho falls, in Borges's eyes, into this category. Indeed, Borges thought that Jews were farmers and businessmen, merchants and shopkeepers but never cowboys; since the age of the horseman in the Pampas began and almost concluded before the Jewish immigration, Gerchunoff's characters, the author of "The Aleph" believed, should be addressed as *chacareros*, small-time farmers descending from the gauchos. This assessment is part of an ongoing controversy. The literary tradition that has the gaucho as protagonist enjoys enormous attention in Argentina. Its highlights in poetry are works by, among others, Bartolomé Hidalgo, Hilario Ascasubi, Estanislao del Campo, and also José Hernández; in nonfiction, it has achieved eminence in numerous books, including a handful written by Sarmiento, William Henry Hudson, Paul Groussac, Leopoldo Lugones, Ricardo Rojas, and Borges; and in novelized form it was a favorite of Benito Lynch and Ricardo Güiraldes.

Most of these literati, if not all, were urban dwellers whose knowledge of gaucho life was confined to sporadic stays on the Pampa. They glorified the gaucho as a quintessential national idol, a courageous peasant always carrying his guitar, his poncho, and his vengeful spirit, which stands in contrast to Gerchunoff's subdued cast: his *gauchos judíos* are not loners but family-oriented breadwinners. They are neither malicious nor rancorous but loyal to their biblical code of ethics. Also, in the works of poets like Hidalgo and Hernández, the narrator is often the gaucho himself, but the prose writers often found strategies to distance themselves from their protagonist. *The Jewish Gauchos,* instead, uses a mix of first- and third-person narration, as well as an omniscient voice serving as an ethnographer with a literary *joie de vivre.* At times the Jewish orphan Jacobo serves as chronicler of the various episodes, but an anonymous "we" occasionally interrupts him, and so does an observer *sub specie æternitatis.* The result is nostalgic and enchantingly lyrical, but isn't *gauchesco.*

In appropriating not only the Spanish language but this most Argentine literary tradition in which to insert himself, Gerchunoff had a clear agenda in mind. Several segments of *The Jewish Gauchos* first appeared, from 1908 on, in the literary supplement of the prestigious newspaper *La Nación,* where Gerchunoff's friend Roberto J. Payró had invited him to work. He was twenty-four years old, and, when he later turned the various segments into a book-long narrative interconnected by its theme and the occasional reappearance of a small set of idiosyncratic characters, he dedicated the whole product "to the revered memory of Baron Maurice de Hirsch. . . . His was the first bread that my people ate on American soil."

According to the Hebrew calendar, the publication of *The Jewish Gauchos* in La Plata, under the imprint of J. Sasé, took place on Passover of 5670. It coincides with the first centennial of Argentina's independence in 1910. Lugones was the person in charge of the cultural part of the national celebration, and apparently it was he who had the idea of turning the scattered reminiscences in *La Nación* into commemorative material. Gerchunoff's enthusiasm was uncontrollable. "As I greet you, my brothers and sisters of the colonies and cities," he writes in the prologue,

> the Republic is celebrating its greatest festival—the glorious feast of its liberation! The days are clear and the nights are sweet, as the praise of national heroes are sung. Voices reach towards a sky that is always blue and white, as in the national flag. The meadows are alive with flowers, and the hills are covered with new grass. Do you remember how, back in Russia, you laid the ritual tables for our Passover's glory? *This* is a greater Passover.

The volume, hence, was meant to be an homage to the national democratic spirit, a wholehearted display of gratitude.

Several Argentine literary works published at the time reflected strong xenophobic sentiments. *Juan Moreira*, an 1880 novel by Eduardo Gutiérrez, portrayed foreigners negatively; and José María Miró (a.k.a. Julián Martel) and Juan Alsina (an important immigration official) were openly anti-Semitic. In their works they criticized Jews in the Pampa for not assimilating. They feared that separatism would ultimately create a nation made of tribes, abysmally fractured. Gerchunoff wisely inserted himself in this debate by using a double edge: he was in favor of neither separatism nor total assimilation; in his eyes, Jews on the Pampa were both in and out. They could *integrate* (the word was his motto) by adopting Argentine national values while also maintaining their religious faith and tradition. And indeed, his argument proved to be successful. Before *The Jewish Gauchos*, immigrants in Argentine letters had been portrayed as outsiders—

Cervantes's tongue a foreign soil, unfriendly and uninviting; after it they became insiders and Spanish became their new habitat.

The issue of belonging to the Spanish language is explored by Gerchunoff in a variety of ways. Early in the book, as the Jews of Tulchin discuss their fate, the possibility emerges of a return to the Iberian peninsula. "Spain would be a wonderful country for us to go to," the Rabbi of Tolno says, "if it were not for the curse of the Synagogue that still lingers over it." At this point the *Dain*, the dean of rabbis, shrugs indignantly, and says in Hebrew: "*Yemach Shemam Vizichrom!* May Spain sink in the sea! May she break into pieces! May her memory be obliterated!" Indictments such as this reappear, and while the Jewish colonists invoke Jehuda Halevi, Maimonides, and other luminaries of Spanish Jewry before 1492, while they relate to Galicians and other Spaniards farming the land north of their colonies, their link to *España* is sour: as one character puts it, "I can never think of Spain without having the blood rush to my eyes in anger and my soul fill with hate."

But Spanish was also the home of Cervantes, Gerchunoff's idol, and that for him was sufficient to reevaluate the ancient Jewish ties to his tongue. His strategy was oblique: he abstracted Cervantes from his milieu and turned him into a unique genius above human affairs. Curiously, he managed to establish a fascinating connection between him and Sholem Aleichem, his other idol. He saw them as an inseparable pair. While humor is not one of Gerchunoff's strengths, his prologue to a 1942 Spanish translation by scholar and lexicographer Salomón Resnick of Sholem Aleichem's *The Old Country,* and a profile of him included in *The Pine and the Palm Tree,* exalt the artistic qualities the Argentine admired most and which he emulated in *The Jewish Gauchos:* the accurate, affectionate descriptions of impoverished popular types. Cervantes, on the other hand, symbolized the very first attempt to make the novel a modern genre; he was also a man of letters devoted to illustrating, by means of plots and action, existential dilemmas. For Gerchunoff, Tevye the milkman was a Yiddish reincarnation of Don Quixote: a humble man whose understanding of reality is limited, yet whose florid imagination and vast (if far-fetched) wisdom allows him to uncover secret truths, an unpretentious figure whose optimism is stronger than the absurdity of life. Both books are mere successions of disjointed episodes but achieve the stature of epics in scope and ambition, a quality Gerchunoff dreamed of achieving as he imagined the multilayered dimensions of the colonies in Entre Ríos.

Actually, Sholem Aleichem and Cervantes are more than idealized models; they are the past and future between which the author of *The Jewish Gauchos* oscillated. When settling in Buenos Aires, at the age of eleven, Gerchunoff dreamed of applying to the Colegio Nacional, of earning a doctorate in letters. His early Spanish readings included *Don Quixote,* handed to him by a journalist friend, as well as books in translation, like *The Thousand and One Nights* and Victor Hugo's novels. References to Cervantes, "our gracious Master," abound in the twenty-six vignettes and continue in all of Gerchunoff's oeuvre, from the book he published after *The Jewish Gauchos,* entitled *Our Master Don Quixote,* to the one he was in the process of drafting when he died; it appeared posthumously as *Return to Don Quixote.* Yiddish was the tongue of Gerchunoff's ancestors, the language of departure and heritage—*der alter shprach;* Spanish, instead, was *la lengua nueva*—the language of the new century, representing renewal but also return. In Gerchunoff's view, Cervantes's masterpiece was the most enduring legacy of Renaissance Spain, a chain linking him to the Iberian peninsula just as the Jews were aborted from its conflicted territory. Sholem Aleichem, on the other hand, was the voice of his people in a more immediate past. Why didn't he choose Yiddish as his literary vehicle? Or perhaps Russian, another tongue important in his childhood? Because he considered himself a citizen of Argentina and wanted fellow Jews to experience a similar feeling of loyalty; because he was a Spanish-speaking Jew in a new land of opportunity.

Prudencio de Pereda's English translation, with an introduction by philosopher León Dujovne, appeared in the United States in 1955 under the imprint of Abelard-Schuman, half a decade after Gerchunoff's death at the age of sixty-six. In spite of being "the first work of literary value to be written in Spanish by a Jew in modern times," it received almost no critical notice. This comes as no surprise: it appeared while the Holocaust and the establishment of the State of Israel were fresh in the mind of its readers, becoming central to the reshaping of an American Jewish identity. The Hispanic world hardly commands any attention from Jewish readers in Europe and north of the Río Grande. Aside from a few stories by Sholem Aleichem, Leib Malach, Isaac Bashevis Singer, and a few other Yiddish writers set in Argentina, the region is considered peripheral and is all but forgotten, even today, in the Jewish collective imagination. Jewish history, like all Western histories, travels from east to west, hardly from north to south. Russia, Central Europe, the Middle East, and the United States are center stage. With only half a million Jews on its soil (the fourth largest concentration after the U.S., the Soviet Union, and Israel), Latin America was then a minor appendix in Jewish history, a hemisphere of banana republics where caudillos fight chaotic revolutions and where Jewish culture remained unformed. The fifties were years of revival and fortification. After the Nazi atrocities, Israel, the Jewish homeland, fought to establish the Jews as "normal" modern citizens, with an army, an autonomous government, and a police force. Meanwhile, American Jews were obsessed with its survival amidst its threatening Arab enemies. Little attention was left to a forty-five-year-old bucolic book about the founding of what looked like a bizarre Argentine shtetl. In spite of Gerchunoff's lifelong struggle toward self-definition, American Jews found his literary endeavors almost inconsequential. This icy reception is in sharp contrast to the enthusiasm with which Gerchunoff's original Spanish edition, published by Joaquín Sesé and with an introduction by the folklorist Martiniano Leguizamón, was greeted with enthusiasm in Argentina. The applause was wide and clear: the writer was seen as a "brilliant interpreter of the provinces," a master crafter whose prose "makes us appreciate nature and man living in total harmony." The book not only has had numerous editions and inspired a 1974 film under the same title, directed by Juan José Jusid, it also inaugurated a literary lineage among Jewish-Hispanic American writers that includes parodies of Gerchunoff by the Argentine novelist Mario Szichman and evocative explorations of utopia in *Comuna Verdad*, a 1995 novel by Gerardo Mario Goloboff about Jewish anarchism in Argentina. These descendants widely expanded the horizons insinuated in *The Jewish Gauchos*. They moved their plots from the province to the city and back to the countryside and continue to investigate the full effect of the marriage between Spanish and the Jewish sensibility.

Gerchunoff is thus the door-opener and path-finder. A consummate and savvy *conversateur*, his stature is not unlike that of H. L. Mencken, the U.S. newspaperman responsible for founding *The American Mercury*. He especially brings to mind Abraham Cahan, the influential editor of the New York daily in Yiddish, *Der Forvert*: Gerchunoff was neither insulting nor tyrannical, but he managed to be both a magisterial man of letters and a meticulous stylist with a passion for verbal quests—not only for the allocutions they exhibited, but for the space they created for new voices. As such he originated an entirely new type in Hispanic American literature: the tongue-switcher *qua* guardian of the language. Gerchunoff spent his entire life in front of the typewriter, so much so that, when death surprised him in 1950, he had seventeen distinguished books to his credit, in addition to *The Jewish Gauchos*; and his reportage, obituaries, literary essays, and articles of general interest were almost countless. (In 1976 Miryam Esther Gover de Nasatsky counted close to 1,300.) Borges was prompted to portray him, in a tribute in the journal *Davar*, as "the perfect friend of the Spanish dictionary"—no small praise for a poor Jewish immigrant from Proskuroff.

With the strength of His arm, God liberated us from Pharaoh in Egypt.
THE HAGGADAH.

prologue

As I greet you, my brothers of the colonies and cities, the Republic is celebrating its greatest festival—the glorious feast of its liberation!

The days are clear and the nights are sweet, as the praises of national heroes are sung. Voices reach towards a sky that is always blue and white, as in the national flag. The meadows are alive with flowers, and the hills are covered with new grass.

Do you remember how, back in Russia, you laid out the ritual tables for our Passover's glory? *This* is a greater Passover.

So, leave your fields, my brothers, and prepare your tables anew! Cover them with white cloths, sacrifice your whitest lambs, and place the wine and the salt at hand. This is a generous roof that shelters us today, that soothes the ancient pains of our race and covers our wounds with the soft salve of motherly hands.

My wandering Jewish brothers, my tortured comrades, now freed men—kneeling, let us raise our faces to that friendly sky's light. Let us join the chorus of praises. Let ours be the words of that Song of Songs that begins:

"Hear this, O ye mortals!"

BUENOS AIRES

Year of the First Argentine Centenary

Argentina is the new Promised Land

one

IN THE BEGINNING   בראשית

*Blessed art Thou, O Lord, single King of all peoples, for
having created the fruits that the soil and the trees give to us!*
DAILY PRAYERS

*The greatest and strongest men of Judea worked the soil;
when the chosen people fell into captivity, they dedicated
themselves to vile and dangerous employments and thus lost
the grace of God.*
RABUSSI

For all its ancient synagogues and great rabbis, the city of Tulchin in
czarist Russia was a dreary place for the Jews. There was a permanent
cover of snow and an equally permanent program of harassment by
the neighboring Cossacks. Then, sixty years ago, the Jews of Tulchin
first began to feel hope at the news of the growing colonies in America. When some visiting rabbi came to preach in the Temple and
brought news, or when the wire dispatches in an Odessa newspaper
spoke of the faraway lands in the Americas, the Israelites would
gather in the house of a prosperous synagogue member and discuss
the prospects of immigration to the New World with true Talmudic
gravity.

   Jacobo remembered those meetings. They were held at a time when
the strange laws of Holy Russia were being multiplied daily. The spears
of the Cossacks were crushing the old walls of the synagogues and
the ancient sanctuaries on whose pinnacles the double triangle of

1

Solomon stood shining—these were carried through the streets in municipal carts. Jacobo would never forget that. He recalled the stirring word of the rabbis, the tears of the women on the day the Cossacks burned the sacred books of the city's leading synagogue— the same synagogue that had been presented to the city by his grand-parents.

The entire Jewish population put on mourning. It was the Eve of Shabuoth, or Pentecost. The palms for the celebration of spring were wrapped in black—as were the figures of the women and children— and the old people fasted for forty days and forty nights. It was then that the *Dain*, the dean of the rabbis, Rabbi Jehuda Anakroi, went to Paris to consult the representatives of Baron de Hirsch about the or-ganization of Jewish colonies in Argentina.

He returned to address a full meeting of the Tulchin Jews, and the old Rabbi was able to make this hopeful announcement: "Baron de Hirsch—may God bless him!—has promised to save us. My compan-ion, Rabbi Zadock-Kahn, has stayed with him in Paris to work out the details." and then the *Dain*, with that eloquence he used so well in synagogue discussions and disputes, began to describe the magnif-icent future he had planned for his persecuted people. His emotional voice rose with his hopes, as it had done in the Temple when he spoke of the Promised Land. He stroked his long white beard with a hand that was knotted and dried from turning the pages of the sacred texts. His small, lively eyes were bright with the visions he described.

"You'll see! You'll see!" he said. "All of you! It's a country where everyone works the land where the Christians will not hate us, be-cause there the sky is bright and clear, and under its light only mercy and justice can thrive."

These words of Rabbi Jehuda Anakroi calmed the spirits of his sad, driven people. Tonight, they looked ghostly in the bright moonlight that poured through the tall windows of the house, so thin and miserable were their features. But the words of the old *Dain* lifted them into near ecstasy, and they almost wept as they answered in chorus: "Amen!"

On Saturday afternoons the most respectable Jews of Tulchin would meet at Jacobo's house for their religious discussions. The *Dain* would clarify many difficult details with the arguments and reasons that he had developed in many memorable controversies. The great Talmudic learning, the lore of the Books of Moses, as well as the laws and the most occult secrets of the Cabala were familiar to him. Many of his listeners felt that these discussions, held in the familiar intimacy of Jacobo's home, deserved a place in those thick volumes, written in the archaic language of the Hasidim, that filled the *Dain's* own bookshelves. (The bookshelves were carved from Jerusalem wood.)

On one occasion, the Rabbi from Tolno had some words of praise for Spain. He spoke of the wonders of that country's climate and, sighing, recalled the days when the people of Israel prospered on Spanish soil.

"Spain would be a wonderful country for us to go to," he said, "if it were not for the curse of the Synagogue that still lingers over it."

The *Dain* shrugged indignantly, and said in Hebrew: "*Yemach Shemam Vizichrom!*, May Spain sink in the sea! May she break into pieces! May her memory be obliterated! I can never think of Spain," the old man said, "without having the blood rush to my eyes in anger and my soul fill with hate. May God in His justice, spread a continual holocaust over the entire earth of Spain as a punishment for having tortured our brothers and burned our rabbis! It was in Spain that the Jews left off cultivating the land and growing livestock. You must not forget, my dear Rabbi, what is said in the Zeroim about life in the country. In that first book on the Talmud, farm life is referred to as the only healthy one, the only life worthy of God's grace.

"That's why, when I heard Rabbi Zadock-Kahn telling me about our emigration to the Argentine, I felt so glad that I forgot about the return to Jerusalem. I recalled a passage from Jehuda Halevi: 'Where happiness and peace reigns, there is Zion!'

"To Argentina we'll go—all of us! And we'll go back to working the land and growing livestock that the Most High will bless. Remember the words of the Good Book: 'Only those who live of their own flock and their own planting have purity of heart and deserve the eternity of Paradise.' If we return to that life, we will be going back to our old mode of life, our true one! May God grant that in my old age I might kiss that soil and, under the light of His true sky, may bless the sons of my sons!"

He spoke for all of us, Rabbi Jehuda Anakroi, this last representative of the great rabbis that had absorbed the wisdom of the Jewish communities in Spain and Portugal. And, as I write his words here, I feel like rushing out and kissing the soil of Argentina, my land of happiness and peace. I want to say with those Jews who had thrilled to his words, "Amen!"

two

THE POET

Favel Duglach was one of the laziest among the colonists. The wheat in his field grew sparse and thin, and the stalks in his neglected corn-field rarely reached the height of one foot. Few hens picked about in his yard, where an old rake and a broken yoke formed part of the dec-oration. The drainage ditch was narrow and shallow and the duck pond was hardly a puddle, but the ducks made a lot of noise, flapping their wings and honking as they flapped about and turned in its muddy water. The fence of his corral was broken and rusted. It was typical, everyone said, of Reb Favel Duglach.

Despite these defects, though, Duglach was esteemed by every-one. He was sensible, kind and wise. He had a thorough knowledge of the Sacred Works and he spent a lot of time in the synagogue, dis-cussing them with the other elders. Duglach could explain every sen-tence of every prayer. He knew the legends that revolved about the ancient prayers and he interpreted them to his friends in full detail.

He embellished these stories with whimsical touches of his own. These were given in his own everyday speech, and such hearty, realistic commentary on the great works seemed to have the ring and touch of true genius.

He spoke to women in wild, passionate dithyrambics, and he had words of praise for the well plowed field and for the neat symmetrical lines of cornstalks bundled and waiting for the threshers.

In other words, Reb Favel Duglach had the soul of a poet, and both the Hebrew and the Gaucho traditions had taken a deep hold on his spirit. This weak, thin Jew, his skin as yellow as a flame, could feel the native Argentine epics of bravery with the same exaltation he experienced when telling some story from the Bible to a tense, expectant group in the synagogue. His eyes shone with brightness, as marked as the yellowness of his skin, and his poor frail body became tensed, vibrant and brave.

He was an original-looking man. A hooked nose dominated his face, and his long beard was balanced by long locks of hair at the back of his head. He wore the loose gaucho trousers, the *bombachas*, under his traditional Jewish cassock, that was belted in his case. It was a fantastic getup, but Favel explained the absurdities by stating: "I'm a Jewish Gaucho."

He was, in fact. In his choppy, aspirate speech, he often glorified the nomadic life of the Gauchos. He knew all the legends of this region and would frequently relate them to his fellow colonists on the Sabbath, interpolating them with his stories of the Bible. The feeling he put into these pieces brought the heroism of the Gauchos of Entre Ríos to life and revived the warlike wrath of the ancient Israelites who fought in the spirited armies of Jephthah and King David, and carried the splendor of their faith and power to the far cities of the Orient. On one occasion, his listeners asked him the meaning of one of the most solemn prayers, and Reb Favel Duglach explained its origin and meaning in this way:

"Our people were held captive in Babylon," he began. "They had their shops on the shores of the Euphrates River and most of their customers were enemy soldiers, still armed with cudgels and crossbows. Near the wall of the city stood their little Jewish temple, displaying the double-triangled star. Inside the city, naked courtesans would dance in front of *their* temple and in the presence of their princes and their priests, but the Jews had confidence in the justice of Jehovah and they directed their prayers to Him. One Sabbath morning, a robust and handsome young Jew knelt before the sanctuary of the temple, and then announced to the Jews that their hour of liberation had come. 'God used His strong arm to take us out of Egypt,' he told them, 'and He will free us from the yoke of this enemy, as well!'

"The young Israelites gathered around him and then they went off to battle. During all that day and that night, the great walls of the city were besieged, and the accursed people trembled at the sounds of clashing shields and the thunder of the Israelite catapults. Our men lifted their hymns of war towards a sky filled with smoke and clouds. At the same time, the old men offered their prayers in Jehovah's Temple. The battle was lost, however; the Babylonian hosts defeated the Israelite avengers.

"The young hero and nine of his comrades fell into the hands of the enemy and suffered martyrdom. With bronze combs, they flayed the skin from the young Israelite's body, broke his arms and his legs and dropped him at the Temple at the very moment of the most sacred prayer.

"The young man made a sign with his eyes and spoke to the Jews. Under that sacred roof, his dying voice resounded like a triumphant call, and he exhorted his brothers to fight for their freedom. His last word left his lips with his last breath, and it seemed to the reverent watchers that this last breath of the hero's formed the specter of a magnificent eagle over his dead body."

As Duglach finished, Rabbi Abraham, the Shochet, sighed. "You speak like a great preacher, Reb Favel," he said to him, "and yet you've never studied at the Yeshiva." Rabbi Abraham was the Shochet of the colony—the ritualistic butcher of the meat—and a very learned man.

"That's true," Favel said. "I could never get on with the instructors. They bored me with their theological interpretations, and they forced me to learn the Scriptures by rote. But—in his own house—my father taught me the true wisdom of the Jews, and it was thanks to the teaching I got from him that I grew to truly appreciate and love life and nature. Maybe that's why the Shochet of Rosch Pina says I'm a heretic—I love all life. I admire the Gauchos as much as I admire the ancient Hebrews. The Gauchos, too, are patriarchal and noble."

Reb Favel never missed a rodeo in the vicinity of Entre Ríos. He loved the true Gaucho scene. The well-tossed lasso, the bucking colts, the deft masterly roping—all brought shouts and exclamations of "Bravo!" from him. He, himself, the thin little Jew, would often take part in the contests, chasing and roping the young bulls on a par with the best of the Gauchos. The most spirited horse became gentle under him; the beast's fire and strength moved only at the direction of his stubborn spurs. On rainy afternoons. Favel Duglach would join the group in Don Remigio Calamaco's tent; he admired and respected the brave old Gaucho whose history was full of typical gaucho deeds.

Sitting with the others around the warming *brasero*, he listened to the Gaucho stories and took his turn at playing the host's battered old guitar. The rain would cover the fields with little pools and the water would pour with a rushing sound into the pasture pond. On those afternoons, Don Remigio's tent was a refuge for the young Gauchos. The singing of regional songs alternated with narrations about local heroes, and on one of these afternoons Reb Favel told the story of a fight between a Gaucho and a tiger. Don Remigio's eyes shone brightly as he listened to the story of this famous happening. His eyes were almost covered by the thick eyebrows, but one could see them glow with the savage emotion he felt. The Jew's words were like short hard blows of a sculptor's mallet as they created the primitive and admirable figure of the story's hero, and made his courage so living and real that the young listeners were moved to shouts of surprise and shock, and then of applause.

The Gaucho's name was Pedro Núñez and, at the story's time, he was a worker on the Galarce ranch, one side of whose land was bordered by a deep, pathless forest.

Tigers and mountain lions abounded in the thick, humid woods, and they would often come out for prey. Pedro Núñez often hunted them on the border. Armed with only a thick-skinned poncho that he wrapped around his left arm as a shield and a dagger held in the right hand, he would take a stand and meet the charge of the aroused beast. Not a muscle of his grim, sun-tanned face would move as he leaned back in the pose of the ancient gladiators, the left arm holding the poncho forward, the right holding the dagger back and ready— his eyes watching and calculating the exact spot from which the hurtling beast would spring.

One day, Núñez wanted to show the sons of the rancher how to hunt a tiger in this courageous way. The boys borrowed guns and horses, and the group set out for the forest. A tiger had been roaming around the border for some time now, and, according to the people who had seen him, he was a hungry tiger.

The group was preceded by their dogs as they went towards a stream at the edge of the forest, and even before they had reached there, the barking dogs had moved into the forest and roused the tiger.

"That's my dog, Blanco," Núñez said. "He can find them."

The shining eyes of the beast could actually be seen through the foliage. They looked like two live coals. The boys pointed their rifles but then something had happened that caused Reb Favel's voice to break with emotion in the telling.

"Just imagine," he said. "No one was actually in danger, because there were four rifles pointed and ready, but the tiger in his first jump leaped upon the dog, Blanco. Pedro Núñez forgot the four riflemen. With a shout that bounded against the wall of trees, he pulled a calf-skin from one of the saddles, took out his dagger and rushed for the tiger.

"The fight lasted only an instant. The four youngsters sat on their horses and watched, silent and helpless. The tiger had raised his head at Pedro's shout, and then got ready to spring before finishing the dog. Pedro hunched himself in the gladiator pose, the skin held up as a shield, the dagger back and ready to strike. The tiger leaped, with a thunderous roar, and then fell at Pedro's feet. The Gaucho's dagger had pierced its heart. Pedro extracted the knife with difficulty—it had entered the beast's chest for one half of its length—then, speaking calmly, as if he had done nothing, he turned to the four stunned young men and said: 'Yes, it was hungry. It was a hungry tiger.'"

The emotion of this story filled Duglach with delight. The courage of the simple Gaucho—the Gaucho of the great tradition—gave the piece a wonderful, simple power for him.

That was another reason why Duglach was loved by all. His spirit could appreciate the real worth of the Gaucho tales as well as the ancient Hebrew stories. He neglected his work and his farming, but he knew the secret of giving life to the ancient grandeur of Israel and the present vigor of the Pampas.

three

THE ANTHEM

During their first years in the colonies of Entre Ríos, the Jews knew very little about the new homeland. Their conception of the Argentine people and customs was a confused one. They admired the Gaucho, and feared him, and they conceived of his life as a thrilling amalgam of heroism and barbarism. They had misinterpreted most of the gaucho tales of blood and bravery and, as a result, and formed a unique conception of their Argentine countryman. To the Jews of Poland and Bessarabia, the Gaucho seemed a romantic bandit, as fierce and gallant as any hero of a Schummer novel. The factory girls in Odessa had avidly read Schummer after their hard day's work. Now, the farm girls in Entre Ríos did the same thing.

In the synagogue—constituted by one or another ranchhouse in Rajíl—the old and young men discussed their ideas about Argentina. The enthusiasm they felt for the free life here—something they'd dreamed about during the dark days in Russia—had not softened a bit. All felt a fervent love for this country, however new and unknown it seemed. The hope they felt was as fresh as the new black earth their plows turned; the new hope and the new earth made their own selves feel new, their bodies young.

On Saturdays, until midday and after, the men would stand at the door of the synagogue—not far from the corral in this instance—and recall their sufferings and exodus, as if the immigration from Imperial Russia had been the historic Exodus of the Bible.

They talked; they argued. José Haler, who had done his military service in Russia, once maintained that Argentina had no army.

"What do you know about that?" Reb Isaac Herman almost shouted at him. Reb Herman was a bent old man, palsied and infirm, who taught the children of the colony their prayers. He opposed José energetically. "You don't know anything, you! You're a little soldier boy, that's all. What do you mean, Argentina has no army?"

"Anybody can understand that, Reb Isaac," José said. "Here in Argentina, the Czar is a President and he doesn't need soldiers to defend him."

"And what about those that we see at the railroad station at Domínguez? What about those, eh?"

The question confused José. It stopped him. He could not satisfactorily explain the presence in Domínguez of the sergeant whose saber in its rusted scabbard was so frightening to the children.

On another afternoon, a neighbor brought news of a coming festival in Villaguay. He told of the arches and flags and banners being erected in the streets of the municipality. This news was commented on everywhere and another colonist proposed that they find out the reason for the festival.

The colonists did not know a word of Spanish. The young men had quickly taken up the dress and some of the manners of the Gauchos, but they could manage only the most basic Spanish phrases in their talk with the natives. It was decided, nevertheless, that their

Gaucho herdsmen, Don Gabino, a comrade of the great Crispín Velázquez and a veteran of the Paraguayan War, should be consulted about the matter. Don Gabino thought that the preparations might be for some local fiesta, or might be for a coming election, perhaps. This idea seems very logical at first, but it was later rejected. Finally, it was the Commissary for the colonies, Don Benito Palas, who cleared up the matter of the preparations for the Jews and explained to the Shochet, in eloquent yet simple form, the full significance of May 25th, Argentina's Independence Day.

The idea continued to interest the colonists of Rajíl, and in the nightly conversations and rest periods of the day they talked about the date. Each one had his own idea about the significance of what had happened on May 25th, but all felt its genuine importance. Finally, it was suggested that the colony celebrate the great anniversary.

It was Israel Kelner who first offered the idea. Israel had once gone to Jerusalem to organize the immigration sponsored by Baron Rothschild. An eminent Hebraist who had been publicly praised by the Shochets of Rajíl and Karmel, Kelner enjoyed great prestige in the colonies, and often delivered the principal address at ceremonies held in the colony. Now, he took a trip to Las Moscas and learned from Don Estanislao Benítez all the necessary details about the 25th of May.

The commemoration of the day was decided upon, and the Mayor and Shochet were designated as organizers for the festival. Jacobo, the Shochet's helper, who was the most acclimated of all the young men, put on his best pair of gaucho pantaloons and rode from house to house on his smart little pony to announce the holding of an assembly that very night in the synagogue.

At the meeting, the details of the celebration were discussed and it was decided first not to work on the holiday, of course, to bedeck the doorways of the houses with flags, and to hold a big meeting in the clearing, at which Reb Kelner would deliver an appropriate speech. It was decided, furthermore, to invite the Commissary to the festival as well as the Administrator of the colonies, Herr Bergmann, a harsh and unsocial German who had little feeling about the occasion to be commemorated.

During the preparations, a further difficulty arose. It was discovered that no one knew the colors of the Argentine flag. It was too late to do anything about it now, and so the preparations had to go on. Finally, the great day came.

The dawn found Rajíl bedecked like a ship: the doorways were covered with flags and banners of all colors. The Argentine colors were there, too, though the colonists did not realize it. A mild sun shone bright but not too warm as it lit up the flat countryside and bathed the yellowed shrubs and the white walls of the huts with its new warmth. The Commissary sent his little band, and they swept into the music of the National Anthem as soon as they arrived at the colony. The hearts of the Jews filled with joy at the sound and, though they were still confused about what this date meant, the thought of this patriotic festival they were celebrating in their new homeland filled their spirits with a new happiness.

The service in the synagogue was attended by all the men and women. Their Jerusalem tunics shown white and resplendent in the sunlit room as they listened to the Rabbi bless the Republic in the solemn prayer of *Mischa-beraj,* a special prayer in praise of the Republic.

After the reading from the Sacred Book, the Mayor spoke. He was a less learned man than the Rabbi, but he knew how to keep people enthralled. He used many gestures of the synagogue preachers, and he would often tear at his chestnut-colored beard.

"I remember," he said, "that in the city of Kishinev, after that most terrible of pogroms, we closed our synagogues. We did not want to have to bless the Czar. Here, in our new country, nobody forces us to bless anyone. That's why we bless the Republic! That's why we bless the President!" Nobody knew who the President was, but that didn't seem to matter.

Immediately after the Mayor's speech, the people left the synagogue and gathered in the clearing. The wild flowers of this season shone brilliantly on an improvised arbor near which the band stood and played the Anthem, lustily and continually. The young men of the colony were showing off their horses, and the native boys from the breakwater district stood in a group, watching silently, but keeping themselves well supplied from the trays of sweets and pastries. The demijohn of wine waited on the arrival of the Commissary for its opening.

It was growing late when Don Benoit Palas appeared with his escort, carrying the Argentine flag. The ceremony began. The Commissary drank his cup of wine and Reb Israel Kelner stood on the dais to speak. In the simple Yiddish of the people, and in the name of this colony, he saluted this country "in which there are no murders of the Jews," and illustrated his feelings with the parable of the two birds—a story that his neighbors had heard on many occasions.

"There was once a bird imprisoned in a cage of iron. He believed that all birds lived as he did, until a certain day when he saw another bird flying freely through space and flitting from tree to rooftop and back again. The imprisoned bird grew very sad; he rarely sang. He thought so much about his imprisonment that he finally got the idea of breaking out and picked at the bars of his cage until he was free."

Jacobo explained the story to Don Benito, who, being a native, could make little of the involved discourse. In his answer to Reb Kelner, Don Benito recited the stanzas of the Anthem.

The Jews could not understand their meaning, but they recognized the word "liberty," *libertad*, and remembering their history of slavery, the persecutions suffered by their brothers and themselves, they felt their hearts beat faster at the word. *Libertad!* It was here. It was theirs. Speaking from their souls, with their truest feelings, they answered the word with one voice. As they did in the synagogue, now they exclaimed together: "Amen!"

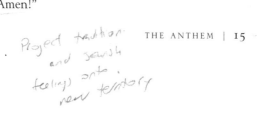

Project tradition and Jewish feelings onto new territory

four

THE SAD AND LONELY ONE

Anyone passing through the village of Rajíl was sure to notice Jeved. Whether he went by in a slow, loaded farm cart or in a swift little sulky, he could not fail to notice that girl; he could not mistake her for anyone else. She was tall and strong, yet beautifully rounded, and when this exciting loveliness aroused much interest, the cold, stern stare of her eyes stopped it dead. She had full erect breasts that pushed against her light smock, rising and falling to the slow yet exciting cadence of her full hipped walk.

She suggested the glorious women of the Bible. Women like Jeved had urged the armies of Jephthah into battle, and in the Holy City, still serene and unmoved, they had assisted at the sacrifices and immolations. Like these women—whose painted portraits still adorned the faded, colored pages of the old missals—Jeved had sun-bronzed hair reaching to her shoulders, making her dark eyes look blacker. In the shadow of such eyelashes, men thought, Solomon must have conceived his sweet songs of peace.

She was a simple girl, of a melancholy turn of heart. The general sadness of this wide, lonely country seemed to reflect itself in her eyes. As she moved along the dew-touched path at dusk, her earthenware jar held on her shoulder, her feet left prints that were light and quick and she seemed a figure out of ancient poetry. Later, at the village well, the young men would drink from her jar while their oxen and dogs waited quietly at the side with the plows and scrapers still warm from the day's work. After, she would refill her jar and turn towards home with the fresh water, her eyes fixing themselves on the grey distance of the road in front of her.

There was something of the priestess in her manner. She answered those who greeted in a slow, grave voice, in the manner of a mystic, not a young beauty. Her words were spoken out of tight, pressed lips, as if they were words of fervent prayer. When a neighbor, walking casually by with his hoe over his shoulder, bid her good-day, Jeved answered: "Good ones! May God send you many good days!" This answer, as always, was like a sacred benediction.

It was thanks to Jeved that the colonists felt the full sense of Nature. With her curved stick, as she moved among the herd to bring out the milking cows, she seemed the perfect picture of the simple peasant. Jeved! The most favored young men were in love with her; they dreamed of pressing themselves on those beautiful breasts; they heard the echo of her voice as sleep came late.

Jeved lived with her parents in a house built on a hillock. In front, the corral and long gates enclosed a yard of all work that was always filled with the crackle of chickens and the barking of dogs. The ditch that drained the rain ran along one side and beyond that a single solitary paradise tree stood like a palm in a desert. Its twisted and leafless branches acquired life in the warmer hours of midday when the larks would come to swing there in the warm winds and make their song the only sound of the siesta hour.

Jeved used to come to the yard to work after the heat of this midday had passed. The sun was redder, but softer, and there was always a breeze. At times, her bare arms would move quietly and rhythmically as she sewed on a cloth spread over her knees; at other times, she would sit and stare at a point on the far sky, with her work in her hands, and darkness would come and surprise her like that. As she stared, her eyes would seem to grow darker and wider—their somberness grew deeper, as did their fascination. If someone approached her at such moments, she would shake herself brusquely and return to her sewing.

This dreaming away of whole afternoons worried her grandmother, who was almost a hundred and who thought the girl might be ill. It worried Jeved's mother, as well. She confided this to her neighbor, the midwife, when she stopped by one afternoon: "I'm fearful about the girl. She spends long hours like that. She doesn't talk, she doesn't hear, and she doesn't see anything. She may be sick—with some strange sickness?"

"Oh, if we only had a good rabbi here!" the midwife said. "A rabbi as smart as the one in Warsaw. As smart as that!"

The old grandmother left off her weaving to correct her. "Not the one in Warsaw," she said in her hoarse, wasting voice. "The one in Vilna—Rabbi Eleazar!—and may these words not disturb him in his tomb! He had a miraculous touch. He was a saint—may he plead for us before God! I've seen him free souls from the worst torments. I've seen him give them rest. Oh, yes!" She turned back to her needles, whispering a prayer that hissed and sibillated through her toothless gums.

The midwife tried to console the two women. She cited similar cases that had turned out well. "After all, my friends, there's nothing to fear. Truly!" she said. "The girl is naturally quiet and doesn't like to go in for fooling of any kind. I don't say that she might not have a small illness—something like water on the stomach, or perhaps a love-sick heart—because she is a beauty! Oh, how beautiful! I wish I had daughters like that. The summer roses and the bread for our festivals don't come out as beautiful as that. May my envy not hurt her! She is so beautiful, she . . ."

Two grateful tears were falling down the wrinkled cheeks of Jeved's mother as she listened. "God bless her, yes!" she said. "Even the doves are not so kind. Oh, what I wouldn't give to be able to kiss her children, to have them as a consolation for my old age! And my husband? He looks into her eyes and says, 'My little jewel, my finest, purest gold, you're worrying me!' And she puts her arms around his neck and chases away his fears with kisses."

The three old women were still talking like that when Jeved came up to get the jar and go for water. They murmured after her as she left: "Oh, lark of my nest!—Joy of my days!—May God keep you!—I would kiss your feet!"

The dog had been chasing the shadows of flying birds. Now, he rushed after Jeved as she called: "Emperor! We're going for water!"

They walked up the path in the first glow of dusk, and Jeved's quiet, somber voice could be heard singing the popular, symbolic song:

> *"With almonds and grapes, I'll reward you;*
> *Sleep, oh sleep, my Israel."*

"Jeved isn't melancholy," they used to say in the colony. "She's just haughty."

The ones who said it loudest were the young men she had rejected. Thus far, Jeved had shown no inclination for any of them. The most gallant and the most daring could not win her simplest smile—not even the rich Liske's son had made any headway, in spite of his pressing insistence.

As a matter of fact, Jeved was neither haughty nor proud. She was humble and industrious; she helped her neighbors in many small tasks. She chatted with everyone, and always took part in the usual talking fests of Rajíl. Certainly, no one doubted her virtue even though she was often seen chatting along with a young man. One morning, Jeved was returning home after taking her father's breakfast out to their wheat field—the old man was scraping it for a new sowing. She stopped to talk to the boy who worked at the breakwater and slapped his face when he added a pinch on her lovely behind to the usual morning's greetings.

At the dances and festivals, Jeved was always surrounded by a crowd of eager young men, but to each one's request for a dance or a stroll she would always give the same "No!"

A man who had been studying at the University of Odessa came to live in the colony and he, too, was struck by Jeved. He courted her, but he had the same lack of success as the others. On Saturday afternoons he would appear at her house, and be greeted warmly and courteously by the family. He had the great distinction of having been to a university—a fact that made all the other girls of the village envious of Jeved—but Jeved would not be impressed. She listened to the man's learned talk, asked him some questions and took part in the discussions he held with her father, but she showed no interest in having him as her betrothed.

The women of Rajíl were saying: "This one is a great man, a learned man!"

"He studied at a University!"

"He still wears a cap with braids, and Jeved doesn't like him!"

Seated on the steps of her house, her chin resting on her hands, Jeved would seem very far away from all the talk. Her face was almost hidden by the sweep of golden hair and her eyes were sad and wondering as she stared at a thing no one else could see.

On working days, she would go to the fields, but in the later afternoon would retire to some quiet spot and lie on the grass to stare at the sinking sun. This daily ritual seemed to quiet her troubled spirit, and she would sink into the vague drowsiness of the afternoon. Bit by bit, she would pick at the memories of her childhood. She remembered a time when she was very young—and very happy. She saw herself running with other children along the golden sands of the beach in the picturesque city on the Black Sea. She was far away from these farms, then. Jeved had never had to think of work—and certainly not farm work. No! The fifteen years she spent in that city were years of pleasure and ease, and the only daydreaming she did then was to dream of the heroes in the novels her father used to read her during the long nights of winter wind and snow. Those years took on a new and unnatural luster now, as she recalled them in the heat of the afternoon sun.

With a sudden twinge of sadness that made her eyes blink and her lips taste of salt, she remembered her first "love." She had swept all other men from her imagination and had made *him* the hero of her dreams. It was he that she talked to in her imagination, as she walked at dusk in her garden, the garden from where the Black Sea could be seen shining beyond the trees.

Sometimes these memories were so real that Jeved felt herself that young girl again. The dead past became alive now—she was in that garden by the Black Sea. After this, the return to reality was always a greater shock. She was filled with a deep melancholy as the dreams of the past faded, as the wonderful, happy moments went irrevocably back and she knew that this was Argentina and that she, Jeved, the hard-working farm girl and might never be anything else. She was reluctant to get up then, to face the harsh country life of the present.

Neither the son of Liske, with his promise of wealth, nor the fine-talking student could replace the dim figure of her schoolmate sweetheart who had promised so much to that younger self of hers. They were both very different from her "love"—they were as hard and coarse as these fields that they worked. Liske, the student, and the brother of the Shochet courted her in a country language, but she remembered the beautiful poetry that the young schoolmate had recited into her ear, his lips almost touching her braid. And what was he doing now? Jeved thought. That young man?

The shadows were deepening around her now, and the bushes surrounding her refuge took on the look of a tropical forest. The cow's mooing was sharp and clear in the sudden purity of the cool dusk. Frogs croaked from a pool nearby and from far, far off, the shouts of the herder announced that it was time to go home.

But the girl Jeved still lay there. What was he doing now? She thought. That fine young man? She imagined him, handsome and triumphant, sought by the women of the city. How she envied those women! Their clothes, their perfumes, their fine, soft skins. They were the friends of her first love, of———? She could not remember his name. Her student! Her sweetheart! She tried a few names, murmuring them to herself, then shook her head each time. It came to her, finally. She remembered it! She said it out loud—and came out of her lethargy and her trance, and got up quickly.

After one such afternoon of dreaming, Jeved was making her way slowly back to the village. Walking along the winding road, she heard the sound of Lázaro's flute behind her. The soft melodious moaning of the simple clay flute had never seemed so sad to her. She stopped and turned and waited for him.

"You're playing like a real musician, Lázaro," she said.

The young man came up to Jeved, with his crippled leg dragging slightly, and smiled at her without taking the flute from his mouth. He continued to play as they walked along together.

Red fringes of the last sunlight reached over the horizon and the country was filled with silence, broken only by crickets' chirps and the momentary barking of the dogs. A quarter moon was beginning to show between the clouds and the first pale stars were starting to appear.

"Why did you stop?" Jeved asked when the boy had taken the flute from his mouth and was walking silently at her side.

"I thought you didn't like my playing."

"Oh, but I do! And especially this afternoon. I do," Jeved said.

Lázaro smiled and began to play again, a softly-drawn-out melody, one of the many from his vast collection of Russian and Jewish songs, the native *vidalitas* and *estilos*. The cripple's tender music flowed about them as they walked along the quiet road. It soothed Jeved so that the troubled memories and dreams of the past began to move away, leaving her quiet and resigned for the first time in many days. She was glad that they were walking slowly; she wanted this peace and communion she felt to last. When Lázaro stopped playing, they walked on in silence and did not speak. Finally, Jeved had to leave.

"They'll be waiting for me at the house," she said. "I have to go. Come this way tomorrow."

Lázaro wanted to say something. He blushed, he looked into the girl's eyes, but his throat tightened and he could not talk. He feared she would notice his embarrassment, and blurted out, "Don't forget to give my regards to Reb Jonas," just to say something—anything.

They separated.

After dinner, Reb Jonas read aloud from a novel of Schummer's. It told of the persecution of the Jews in Spain, a subject that had always moved Jeved. She thought of the protagonist, the famous Don Pedro de Parera, whom the author dressed in velvet and set to mingling among the princes and princesses of the court of the Philips. She frowned as she thought how different men are in life from men in books. How must this Don Pedro de Parera have been in real life? What kind of a man was that first sweetheart of hers? What was he like now? As she asked herself this, she tried to recall the clear picture she once had of him—but his features were dimmer now, and she could not remember him well.

She slept deeply that night. In her dreams she still heard the softly tentative melodies of Lázaro's clay flute. As in the afternoon, they seemed to soothe her yearnings.

The next day, as she lay resting in her quiet refuge, she felt calmer and much less troubled. Would Lázaro come this afternoon? She wondered. She didn't know too much about him because she had never paid any heed to this quiet and brooding boy. How wonderfully he played! On a simple clay flute! The figure of Lázaro, with his lame leg, was painting itself firmly on the foliage that surrounded her retreat, on the blue sky, on the thick shrubbery and on the black earth of the furrowed fields that ran off into the distance.

She remembered, once, how a calf of Lázaro's had broken loose from its halter and how pained she had been by the sight of him chasing that animal, his lame leg dragging behind. She had rushed after the calf and caught it, and she remembered how moved and embarrassed Lázaro had been when she brought the animal to him—so much so that he could not even stammer out his thanks. Her pity warmed her now, as she thought of that day.

Jeved compared Lázaro to the other young men who courted her—the ordinary Liske, the so talkative, so nimble student. Neither of them was worth as much as Lázaro and his wonderful simplicity. He had never said a word to her, but she remembered him looking after her with sad and eager eyes.

Would he come this afternoon? The fact that she had any doubts about this made her angry, and she realized how impatient she felt.

She could think of nothing else now. The moment she heard the first shouts of the herder as the movement towards home began, she jumped up. Then, as she heard the first tremulous notes of Lázaro's flute, without realizing what she was doing, she started to run towards the road, stretching out her arms and crying happily: "Lázaro! Lázaro!"

five

THE FIRST FURROW

The wind is shaking the distant magueys, and it is cold. There's a fine fog dimming the rays of the sun and holding the morning back. The flat tract of field looks white with the morning frost—so white it seems to be snow. But, further on, we know there are neighbors already working, and in the moments when the wind is calm we can hear the noise of the little plow wheels.

We have to mark off a new field for plowing. We've hitched up the most docile oxen and placed the little red signal flag five hundred meters from the spot we start at—the place at which we are all standing now. We'll plow two furrows—one going toward the flag, one returning. Cutting the first furrows in a field is always a solemn occasion. Everybody realizes this.

The two oxen seem to be even more serious than usual this morning. they are munching slowly and rhythmically as they stand yoked to the plow, waiting for the start. Barbos, the dog, realizes the serious occasion more than anyone. The family is out en masse; this is too interesting a morning to stay in the house, no matter how cold it is outside. Mother is holding a jug filled with hot coffee and milk, and the girls are huddling close to her. We boys go about making our preparations.

"Are we ready?"

"Ready!"

I guide the oxen and my brother steadies the plow. "Right!" I shout, then, "Left!" The oxen understand the importance of this first furrow and they move with slow, careful steps. The red signal flag is in a direct line with the chain hanging from the middle of their yoke, a good solid yoke of *quebracho*, made in the colony's carpentry shop on the days when the rain kept us in from the fields.

The plow groans and crackles, digging at the hard earth, and behind it march my mother and sisters, watching attentively, walking solemnly. The dog, Barbos, walks in front of the oxen, wagging his tail and moving his head to the rhythm of their trudging walk. Barbos has a steady good humor; he is also an experienced farmer so that he can appreciate fully the importance of today's plowing. So he goes on, without bothering with the frequent quail flying about.

The oxen pull with their usual resignation and with today's new feeling of cooperation. Their heads are strained forward in the effort but they hardly seem to feel the yoke strapped so ignominiously to their great necks. Two long slivers of foam hang from their lips. The earth that had been so enclosed in winter's frost exhales a strong smell of moisture as it bursts open and the family breathes in this odor as if it were the sweetest aroma. The single wheel of the plow is singing the psalm of full harvests, and in the nearing distance the red flag is waving with the pride of a true standard.

six
FRESH MILK

Close by the little stockade, the girl sat milking. The cow was as gentle as soft bread and stood quietly; her little calf, meanwhile, wandered a few feet away, its legs entangled in its lead cord, and munched at the short grass.

The dawn was rising, with fingers of orange and red beginning to slip over the horizon's edge. In the colony, people were coming awake. The corrals were being opened, and men with long great beards were appearing in the ranchhouse doors, mumbling the prayers of the morning. With the dawn—God's dawn for which the prayers of the holy Rabbis thanked and praised Him—the usual morning conversations began.

"Shall we rake today, Remigio?"

"No, Don Ephraim. It's rained too much. It would be better to plow today."

"Good. Have some *maté*. We'll yoke Chico and the Ugly One for the plowing."

In the clear morning air, a shout is heard from next door.

"Is someone going to the station, Don Ephraim?"

"Yes, my boy is going."

"Will he ask at the grocery if there's a letter for me?"

Meanwhile, by the little stockade, Raquel went on milking the quiet cow. She was on her knees as her fingers squeezed the magnificent udders and pressed out streams of steaming milk. The dawn around them now was the pale red of autumn, but the open neck of Raquel's dress showed full firm breasts that a hot summer sun had baked the color of golden fruit. The milk squirted into the pail with the same soft rhythm as the girl's breathing and the light snorting of the cow.

Raquel's hair falls to her shoulders in dark waves, and the lovely contours of her body are outlined in the light percale dress: the full, fruitful hips, the rhythmic sweep up to the breasts and arms, as in the artistic amphorae of ancient times. The morning light pours over the complacent back of the animal and bathes Raquel's face. Her eyes have the blue artists paint in the eyes of Northern girls and her nose ends in a little bronzed snub.

Raquel, I see the majestic women of ancient Scriptures in you! In the peace of the Argentine plain, you suggest the Biblical heroines who tended gentle flocks in the flat lands of Judea, who sang the praises of Jehovah in the Temple. Raquel, you are Esther, Rebecca, Deborah or Judith. You work beneath a kindly sky and your hands tie golden stalks of wheat into sheaves as the sun basks over the broad field that your brothers sowed and your father blessed. He is neither a money lender nor a martyr now, as he was in czarist Russia.

The life of ancient Jordan is restored now, as you milk the gentle beast and watch over its tender calf. All around you, the ranchhouses are coming alive in morning chores; near you, in the midst of the colony, the swift little stream is offering its morning freshness to an ox and a horse. And, just as in ancient Jerusalem, your father prays to the God of Israel, Commander of all armies, Master of the air, the light and the land, greeting Him in ancient Hebrew: "*Baruch attu Adonai* . . . Blessed art Thou, O Lord!"

seven

THE SHOWER

The afternoon is fading into a sweet, peaceful night. The sky is
streaked with the last yellow sunlight. The animals have sensed the
time and make for the corrals; the people begin to move towards rest.
Out in the fields, the arms of the stilled plows recall the frames of
lyres, and at the spring the bell about the mare's neck tinkles softly
as she leans forward to drink.

The old people are murmuring the evening prayers through closed
lips. A father asks: "Has Juan come back?"

"No, he's gone to pick up the saddle the butcher borrowed."

"And Rebecca?"

"She's washing her hair."

"La Rosilla?"

"Tied up and well."

Actually, the cow, La Rosilla, tied to the corral fence, was shaking
her head sadly.

The shower came suddenly and unexpectedly—and the bright shining sun made diamonds of the raindrops that broke softly and silently as they stuck the ground. Someone shouts: "The calf! The calf!"

Rebecca suddenly appears, running towards the calf that has broken loose and is making for its mother. The girl reaches him as he bites excitedly towards an udder. Rebecca is only partially covered by the towel she has thrown around herself, and the rain falls on her sturdy breasts, on her youthful body strengthened by work. With her full black hair plastered to her shoulders, she looks like a rustic goddess.

eight

THE SIESTA

It is the Sabbath—the day of holy rest, the day so blest in the rabbinical studies and so honored in the prayers of Jehuda Halevi, the
poet. The colony relaxes in warm drowsiness. The white walls and
the yellow straw roofs of the houses shine in the warm benign sun on
a country summer. The sky is cleansed by last night's rain, and it holds
a religious peace and clarity. The earth, though, has a pleasant, living odor. The orchards are in bloom, and the country is an endless
green. In the pasture's center, the little spring erupts with ambitious
freshness and pushes at the green borders of the pool with bursting
ringlets; the sound of its gurgling is like a song. On the highway, covered in a thick shroud of dust, the body of a dead snake looks like a
grappling hook of mud.

The beasts are resting in the pasture. The oxen munch and shake
their heads, as if in thought, while the bright sunlight shatters into
streaks of blue on their horn-points. For the oxen, too, the Sabbath is

a blessed day. Over in a corner, the mare's bell tinkles as she shakes her head and trots to nuzzle her piebald colt rolling on his back in the grass.

The Shochet's house is absolutely quiet. Rabbi Abraham is asleep, as are the children—there are still hours to go before afternoon prayers. The young helper, Jacobo, the orphan of the neighborhood, is braiding his pony's tail. The soft wind balloons his wide gaucho trousers, and his belt holds a shining dagger and a small, lead-weighted *boleadoras*, the native lariat. The grandmother is sitting outside in the shade, with her granddaughter on her lap. The grandmother is very old, and a full kerchief covers her white hair. Her skin is bronzed, and wrinkled with past suffering. She sighs as the little girl sings.

"Jacobo," she yells at the boy. "Leave the pony. Today is the Sabbath."

"You don't think this is work, do you, Doña Raquel?"

"Yes, it is—no matter how much you like it. One must rest on the Sabbath. Hasn't Abraham taught you that?"

The little girl is humming, and singing in a low voice:

> *Weep and moan, oh, you daughters of Zion!*
> *Weep and moan with us . . ."*

"Grandmother," she asks now, "do you know that song? I've never heard you sing it."

"Yes, I know it, child. Look, your head is dirty."

"It was washed yesterday."

"But it's dirty."

Slowly and carefully, she feels and prods with her fingers in the child's hair. "You see? Here's one!" A little clicking sound comes as she snaps something between her nails. "Two—three—four—my poor child! There are so many!"

"Grandmother, tell me that story about Kishinev." (Kishinev had been the scene of one of the worst massacres of the Jews, the girl says.) Meanwhile, she continues to hum the psalm.

"Here's another! They haven't washed your head well at all, child."

"And the song about the shepherd, Grandma?"

"It's very beautiful, Loved One. Have you learned it yet?"

"Rebecca taught it to me."

The grandmother continues her searching in the blonde hair while the child sings in a low voice:

"*There was once a young shepherd in Canaan* . . . Grandma, tell me the story about Kishinev. Do you remember it?"

"Yes, child. Yes, I remember . . . Here's another—look! They washed your head very badly—it's full of lice. One little louse, two, three . . . Look at this one, how big he is! They would eat you, if I didn't clean them out."

"Don't the Scriptures say that you mustn't kill living things?"

"Yes, my child."

"Well, then?"

"Cows are living things too, and still your father sacrifices them."

Don Zacarías is passing just then. He stops to greet the old lady. "Good Sabbath, Doña Raquel!"

"Good Sabbath, and a good year, Reb Zacarías! You've caught me in a bad moment. I see they've washed my little granddaughter's hair very badly."

"That's bad. We have to care for the children, Doña Raquel. What would we do without them?"

"God help us, Reb Zacarías. Children only love their parents after they're gone."

"Isn't that so! A wise man said, 'Children miss their parents after they leave as the cut flower misses the branch.' Hey there, Jacobo! Have you forgotten that it's the Sabbath?"

"I'm not working, Reb Zacarías. I'm just cleaning my horse. I've fixed him up with food and drink, and I want to have him ready to ride to pasture tonight."

"But you're not even supposed to clean him."

"Doña Raquel is cleaning Miryam's hair."

"Oh, let that Gaucho be," Doña Raquel cut in. "He has an answer for everything. Look at him! The complete Gaucho—those awful pants, the belt, the knife and even those little lead things to kill partridges with. But, see him in the synagogue and he's quiet as a mouse. He doesn't even know his prayers. Imagine! Educated by my son, the Shochet, and he doesn't know how to pray."

"Well, that's how they are these days, the young ones. Have you heard the latest news about that certain one?"

"What news? Tell me."

"Well, the daughter in a certain house . . ." and with a deprecatory look, Zacarías nodded towards the little yellow house of Ismael Rudman.

"Oh, yes. Abraham told me about that. It's a shame. Is it certain? Is it a fact?"

"It is—unfortunately. Reb Ismael didn't attend the synagogue this morning, and he was supposed to read the chapter. Later, we found out through my brother what happened. *She* ran away with the Gaucho. A Gaucho!"

Jacobo interrupted at this point. "Remigio's a good boy," he said. "He taught me to ride and to use the lariat."

"Do you see how it is?" Doña Raquel exclaimed. "It's all the same to this renegade. It's just as if she'd gone away with a Jew!"

The voice of the village shepherd starts to call from afar; evening is coming on. At the door of the house, the venerable figure of Don Abraham appears. He puts on his short tunic; its fringes flick over the head of his mother.

"Good Sabbath, Rabbi Abraham!"

"Good Sabbath and a good year, Reb Zacarías," he answers. "What other news do you have about this morning's occurrence?"

"We should have seen it coming. She used to make tea in the samovar on the Sabbath, and she ate chicken slaughtered by the

Gaucho. She was lost! Long before this, she was lost. Do you think it's time to go to the synagogue?"

Rebecca comes out of the house and sits at the side under the eave. Her hair is disheveled from sleep and her first greetings are in a hoarse, croaking voice. Jacobo is bored with the pony now, and begins to sharpen his dagger on the stone. Hearing Rebecca outside, he begins to sing in the way Remigio had taught him: "*Oh, my dream . . .*"

nine

THE NEW IMMIGRANTS

The morning the new immigrants were expected, some two hundred
people went to the station at Domínguez. The immigrants were expected on a ten o'clock train, and their colony was to be established
outside San Gregorio and close to the forest where, according to local
legend, cattle thieves and tigers abounded.

Spring was coming everywhere, and the green fields of the meadows were already well dotted with daisies.

The station was crowded and the people speculated about the new
arrivals from Russia, especially about the Rabbi from Odessa, an old,
learned Talmudic scholar of the Vilna Yeshiva who had been to Paris,
it was said, and had been very courteously received by Baron de Hirsch,
the Father of the colonies.

The chief and the sergeant of the Villaguay constabulary had come
to the station to assist in the arrival, and were talking quietly together.

Other Gauchos were there, playing jackstones while a number of the Jewish colonists watched.

The Shochet of Rajíl had drawn the Shochet of Rosch Pina into a discussion in the hope of confusing him before so many people. They were talking about the Rabbi among the expected immigrants, and the Shochet of Rosch Pina was telling some things about him. He had known him in Vilna where they studied the sacred texts together. The new Rabbi was a fine person and he knew the Talmud almost completely by memory. He was a member of the group that had gone to Palestine to purchase lands before Baron de Hirsch had thought of launching this project in Argentina.

The man had never practised as a rabbi, the Shochet said. After he finished his studies, he had become a merchant in Odessa, but he often contributed to *Azphira,* a periodical written entirely in ancient Hebrew.

Later, the two Shochets debated a complicated point of domestic law, and the Shochet of Rajíl quoted an idea of the divine Maimonides on the sacrifice of bulls.

Awaiting the new arrivals recalled deep and lasting memories for most of the crowd. Many remembered the morning on which they had fled the unhappy realm of the Czar. Then they recalled their arrival in this promised land, in this new Jerusalem they had heard proclaimed in the synagogues and had read about in the circulars carrying little verses in Russian, praising the soil of this country:

> "To Palestine, to the Argentine,
> We'll go—to sow;
> To live as friends and brothers;
> To be free!"

"Don Abraham," the sergeant said to the Shochet, "here comes the train."

A sudden rush of talk spread. Behind the hills, in the clear morning, the thread of the engine's smoke was seen.

When the train puffed in, the immigrants descended from two coaches. They looked drained and miserable, but their eyes shone with bright hope. The last to descend was the Rabbi. He was a tall, broad old man with a pleasant face and a thick white beard. The colonists gathered around him; he was overwhelmed with greetings and wishes of welcome. The Shochet of Rajíl, Don Abraham, worked his way to the Rabbi's side and took charge. He led him away from the station. They were followed by the colonists and the long line of immigrants, with their bundles and their children. The immigrants seemed to be losing some of their misery as they moved in the soft morning air and stared at the beautiful countryside.

When the lines had moved a little away from the station, Don Abraham mounted the stump of a tree and made a speech of greeting—well interspiced with Hebraic quotations. The new Rabbi answered for the immigrants with the quotation of a short verse from Isaiah. He spoke about czarist Russia then, telling of the horrible sufferings of his people there.

"Here," he said, "we shall work our own land, care for our own animals, and eat bread made from our own wheat." The Rabbi was filled with a thrilling enthusiasm, and he made an imposing and prophet-like figure with his great beard waving in the wind. When he stepped down from the stump, the Rabbi embraced the sergeant and kissed him warmly on the mouth.

Then, in the full warmth of the morning sun, the caravan started for San Gregorio.

ten

THRESHING WHEAT

It was still morning when the workers tied up the last sack of wheat. The threshing machine stopped, and the people went and sat in the shade of the unthreshed bundles and had coffee. A fierce sun was burning. It poured its heat over the dried countryside and gave it the gold-brown look of toast.

Far off, in the pasture, among the gullies and small pools, the oxen moved slowly and sadly, unmindful of the constantly chattering dogs.

The Mayor of the colony, an eloquent and astute old man who had been elected by his neighbors assembled int he synagogue, was talking of the results of the harvest in general, and of the beauty of our wheat in particular.

The Mayor was almost illiterate, but he had memorized many quotations from the Scriptures and he would always cite an apt one, whether he was handing over a new plow to some colonists or buying wire for the pasture fence. On this hot morning, surrounded by his friends and neighbors, in the shadows of the what bundles, he spoke to us about the advantages of country life.

"I know very well," he said, "that we are not in Jerusalem. I know very well that this land is not the land of our forebears—but here we plant seed, and here we grow wheat, and at night, when we come in from the fields, wheeling our plows, we should thank the Most High because He had led us from the place where we were hated and persecuted, where we were miserable."

"The wheat of Bessarabia is whiter than this wheat of the colony," the Shochet answered him. He paused to show his discontent. "It's true," he said, "in Russia we lived badly, but there was the fear of God there and we lived according to the Law. Here, the young people are turning into Gauchos."

The noise of the thresher starting broke into this sad commentary. It was now Moisés Hinteler's turn to have his wheat threshed. He stood quietly beside the rolling, roaring drum of the machine. He was short and thin, but his little round myopic eyes had a look of true happiness. His wife stood watching at his side. She, too, was prematurely aged from the miseries suffered in czarist Russia. Their daughter, Deborah, an active, robust girl, was preparing the lunches.

The work began, and we mounted the pile of wheat to get at the top bundles. The machine was soon roaring and spitting.

"Moisés!" the Mayor shouted. "Did you have bundles of wheat in Vilna, hey? Remember how you worked as a jeweler, fixing old watches and earning one or two rubles a month? And look now, Moisés—you have land, wheat and livestock!"

He lifted his cup in a toast. "As we used to say in Russia, Moisés: May your land be always fertile, and may the fruit of your orchards be so plentiful that you can't gather it all!"

Moisés remained standing quietly by the machine. Memories of his unhappy life in Vilna rushed about his head. He remembered the martyrdom and sorrow of being a Jew there.

The big drum of the thresher began to shoot out grain, and the wheat fell like a golden rain in the bright light of the blessing sun. Moisés slowly extended his hand and held it, palm upward, in the golden shower. He held it there for a long time. At his side, his wife's face was brightening; his daughter was watching him happily.

"Do you see this, oh mine?" the old man said. "This wheat is ours."

Tears spurted from his eyes and ran down his sad, beaten face. They merged with the pouring grain that a worker was already gathering into the first sack.

live from the land
be productive
pride

eleven

THE PLUNDERED ORCHARD

It was a clear, warm day. From both sides of the village, the green fields of corn stretched far, and the tall stalks waved ever so slightly in the warmish breeze. The boys were bringing the animals out into the big clearing that separated the two lines of cottages, preparing to take them to pasture.

The colony found itself in a period of rest immediately preceding a new plowing and seeding. We all went to the synagogue that day— it was the anniversary of a neighbor's death, and his sons had to say the prayers for the dead prescribed by ritual law.

Later, a local dispute was taken up in much detail, and the Mayor worked for a reconciliation between the contending parties. The Shochet held forth with much Solomon-like reasoning and cited some very impressive decisions on similar disputes in the past. After an exciting exchange of insults, in which the various scandals in both families were embellished and distorted, peace was made and the enemies reconciled.

Some of us decided to go to town that afternoon, and the reconciled disputants each gave us some errand.

"Bring me some post cards."

"Bring me that rice I bought at the grocer's Sunday."

Our family left the synagogue together. The sky was very blue and it seemed very low today, but the sun was full and warm and, as we walked, we could see how it drenched the fullblown orchards directly in back of the white or straw-walled cottages. There were few big trees on the street of the colony. Our house had a solitary paradise tree in front of it, and today the cup of is shadow was small and black.

Turning to go into the house, we noticed a small grey cloud on the far sunlit horizon.

"It might rain," someone said.

"It might," our Gaucho helper said. "Yes."

About noon, the cloud grew bigger. It was spreading out; its greyness got thicker.

"Let's ask Don Gabino about it," the Mayor said. But Don Gabino, the chief Gaucho worker in the colony, was out in a distant pasture with the livestock. The old Gaucho, who, according to legend, had served with Crispín Velázquez, the great Liberator, as the local astronomer and meteorologist, and his predictions were never wrong.

Lunchtime came and everyone had to go in to eat. The people retired with an uneasy feeling. Meanwhile the cloud continued to grow ont he golden blue horizon. It spread, and it seemed to come close to the ground.

The colonists were accustomed to all kinds of natural phenomena— and disasters—but still they grew more and more worried about this cloud that had come on without wind or thunder. Some of the more daring and talkative of the colonists mounted the roofs to watch the phenomenon, but they could not or would not explain it. They watched in silence.

Nobody was thinking of going to town now, and nobody thought for even a moment about the local quarrel that had been patched up this morning at the synagogue by the Shochet after the orphans had recited the last prayer in memory of their father.

Everyone was watching the cloud as it spread and invaded the sky. It moved toward us slowly. An hour later it fell on our village—the heavy stinking flight of LOCUSTS!

"The plague!" the Shochet shouted. "The plague of the locusts!"

"To the orchards! To the orchards!"

Everyone swept to the defense. The sun was obscured by the frightening thick cloud, and the paradise trees, the corral posts and all other standing things were covered with thick blankets of the insects as their odor spread around us. The orchards were filled with grey, moving stains.

The men and women and the children rushed into the flight, beating on cans and rattling coins to frighten away the terrible plague. Some shouted at the locusts, but without any visible results. The locusts were eating the beans, the flowers, and even the thin little streaks of dog's grass. Women were weeping and hitting angrily at the pests with cloths.

"Raquel, your plant!" a boy shouted.

Raquel was back in the orchard, but she threw down the purse she had been rattling and rushed to where the boy stood. Locusts swarmed over her beloved plant, her magnificent rosebush.

"A cloth! A cloth!" Raquel cried. "Someone help me!"

No one paid any attention. In her excitement, she did not think of rushing into the nearby house for a cloth—any cloth—to shield her rosebush, but quickly took off her blouse and wrapped it around the beloved plant. Her skin was nut-brown and her young breasts pushed against her sweat-sodden undershirt. After she had wrapped the plant carefully, she wiped the sweat from her face with the ends of her long blonde hair.

"Raquel!" Moisés called. "Come and help! Come!"

The girl was so tired she could hardly stand erect, but she moved slowly and surely into the orchard. The terrible fight lasted for hours— hours full of shouting, noise-making and hitting back at the pests. But the orchards were left bare and the locusts headed for the wheat fields.

The sun was going down, and the air was a little cleaner now. We went back towards the house, saddened and ashamed. The Shochet was mouthing curses as he began to say the first prayers of the evening, and when Don Gabino got back with the animals, only the tired sobbing of women and the barking of dogs could be heard in the quiet colony.

twelve

THE SONG OF SONGS

How much better is thy love than wine!

The boy found Ester not far from the draw well. She was cutting melons among the full, bending corn stalks. She knelt on the thick floor of melon leaves and flowers as she worked, and seemed to glow in the heat of the sun and the flare of the sunflowers.

She bent her head when she saw Jaime, moving the cut melons aside with her hand and surreptitiously letting down her skirt that she'd bunched at the waist to have her legs free. She felt her cheeks coloring and her voice seemed to catch in her throat as she greeted him. "Finished for the day? So early?"

Jaime did not answer her. Sitting straight on his horse, he heard her voice but not her words. He was staring eagerly at the girl's fine profile, at her disheveled hair, her panting full breasts. When she looked at him for a quick moment he saw the dilated dark eyes that were as black as fine earth plowed soon after rain.

Ester knew the reason why he had suddenly appeared. Jaime had been after her for a long time now. The songs he sang at the colony feasts were for her alone, as were the feats and stunts he performed in the rodeos. She was not displeased with this daring young man who was as hard and straight as a fine young tala tree and as agile as a squirrel.

Her embarrassment was passing now, and she looked up at his sunburned face. "You're through for the day."

"Look at this, Ester!" he exclaimed without answering. He bent awkwardly and held out his open hand. There were some things in it that she could not make out at once.

"What are they?"

"They're for you."

They were partridge eggs he'd found on one of the hillocks. Ester took them, and to see that she held them carefully the boy got down from his horse.

"Don't hold them like that. They'll break."

Ester had knelt to wrap them in a leaf, and as Jaime bent over her his cheek was brushed by her hair. Ester could feel him tremble. "Ester," he began . . .

He stopped, and they knelt in silence. Ester was not as perturbed as before, but she tried to hide any excitement she felt. She could think of nothing to say, though.

"The corn is very tall," she said, finally.

"Yes, it is."

"But look at Isaac's . . ."

"Ester," Jaime began again. "Ester, I have to talk to you."

Ester lowered her head and picked at some leaves. Her hands were trembling.

"They tell me," Jaime went on, "that you intend to get married to a boy from San Miguel. Do you know who told me? Miryam. No, it wasn't Miryam, it was the Mayor's sister-in-law."

"That one! It would be she," Ester said. "She wants me to get married to her cousin, the cripple."

"And they tell me that the father of this boy would give you both two pair of oxen and a cow."

Ester shook her head, but Jaime went on. "What's your idea in all this, Ester? How do *you* feel?"

"I don't know, yet."

"I came here today, Ester, to tell you that I want to marry you."

The girl did not answer at once and Jaime repeated what he had said. He repeated it again, and then she said in a low voice: "Speak to my father. I don't know."

A slight breeze stirred at the tall stalks and some leaves of the sunflower fell over Ester's hair. One slipped to her throat and reflected its pure yellow on her skin. She brushed it off and straightened up. "I must go back," she said.

"I will go with you," Jaime said.

As they stood up together, Jaime drew her to him in a tight, crude embrace and kissed her hard on the lips. The sound seemed loud in the quiet field, and as Jaime released her he let his arms fall and stood staring at Ester with a surprised, pleased look on his face.

They said nothing. Jaime mounted his horse and they started for the village at a slow, leisurely pace. Before they came to the house, Ester looked up at him and said: "Oh, how they'll envy me!"

"And me, too! Listen, I'm going to break in my little white mare for you."

When they came to the house, Jaime called her father outside and began his proposition: "You know that my land is right next to yours, Reb Eleazar, and so . . ."

thirteen

LAMENTATIONS

Weep and wail, O daughters of Zion!

The women were meeting in Don Moisés' house to recite the lamentations required by ritual. These were the days set aside to recall the loss of Jerusalem, and Don Moisés' house was one of the most respectable in Rajíl. The colony had a sad, mournful air these days, and the significance of this time had deepened the wrinkles in the faces of the old people.

Outside the house, the old men sat silently on two long wooden benches. It was a typically clear Argentine night and the moonlight flooded their sorrowful faces, their long beards and their big knotty hands. They seemed to form a mystic frieze of the Apostles. Who can forget those burning anguished profiles that we have seen so often in ancient stonework or on the walls of churches?

Look at Moisés! You, Don Moisés, with your bent back, your weary feet and your sad, deep eyes! How much you resemble the figures of the saintly fishermen who accompanied Jesus—Jesus, your enemy Jesus, the disciple of Rabbi Hillel, your master. These friends of Jesus know of your sorrows. Like you, they dipped their bread in their tears when they remembered the pains your brothers suffered, the lashings in all the cities, the kicks on all the roads of the world. Old Moisés, your pallid face—as furrowed by sorrows as is the land of your sons by their plows—yours is the face whose eyes lit up at the Good Tidings long ago in the wonderful Temple, when the virgins raised their bare arms towards the sanctuary and men came from far ends of Judea, carrying lambs and doves to sacrifice to God in celebration of the Passover.

Like the roaring words of that dying hero in the synagogue during the Captivity, your sighs will spread their sad music under this amiable sky and over this wonderful land now responding to the rhythm of the *vidalita*, to the sighs of love and the mooing of happy cows. Just as then, no one will answer your lament, and if Jehuda Halevi, his head covered with a sack of ashes in token of sorrow, were to enter Jerusalem now and recite his elegy, the Saracen would crush him again under his horse's hooves.

"Shall we pray now, Mother?"

"It's still early. We have to wait for the Shochet's wife, her sister and the midwife."

"The midwife—I like that!" an old woman exclaimed. "Why, she doesn't even know how to read. You have to say the words for her first, and then she repeats them."

"And to hear the way she cries, one would think she had composed the prayers herself."

"There are a lot of them like that," said Moisés' wife. "They can't read one letter of the *Majzor*, the prayer book, but, on the other hand, they do really feel. Oh, yes, my friend, one learns to read with the heart."

The men came into the house.

"We'll say the evening prayers first," Moisés proposed, "and then the lamentations."

"Are there ten men?"

"There are fourteen of us."

"Let's begin."

Facing east, Moisés began with the memorable words: *"Baruch attu Adonai!* Blessed art Thou, O Lord!"

After the evening prayers were said, the women sat on the floor opposite the men and the lamentations began. Their mouths, twisting into sour grimaces, groaned out the aged complaints of the race into the quiet, spellbinding night. Tears like raindrops fell on the pages read by candlelight, while outside, the dogs joined in the moaning with their long, deep howls.

"Like the wife who is certain her husband will never return . . ." chanted the voice of the Shochet, "Jerusalem, like a woman who does not know her husband's fate, tears at her clothes, bites at the earth and loosens her hair to the wind; so art thou, Jerusalem, promised land, now desolated and humiliated by thine enemies."

"So art thou, O Jerusalem," the women repeated in voices shaken with sobs, and then howled out lament into the quiet darkness.

In the patio outside, Rebecca was talking to Jacobo.

Her blue eyes, her glorious hair and thrilling young body were exciting the boy. "And why aren't you praying?" he said.

"I'm too young. When I get married, I'm going to pray with the others."

"Yes, that'll be better."

"What do you mean?"

"Well, I mean that I'll be with you, then," Jacobo said.

"You're with me almost all day now."

Jacobo was about to answer when the sudden screaming of the women inside interrupted. Then the voices of the men continued the lamentations. The steady chorus recalled the glory of Jerusalem—

Ieruschulaim, Dais of Wisdom, Throne of Justice, Kingdom of the Prophets. The words continued lamenting the eternal poverty of Israel. The dogs howled outside with their faces lifted toward the moon.

"Rebecca," Jacobo was saying, "they tell me you have a boyfriend."

"It's not so. That must be one of your stories."

"But you would like to have one."

Rebecca didn't answer. Jacobo took her hand. He sensed the beauty all around him, that miraculous sky of Entre Ríos, and, putting his arm around the girl, he pressed her to him and timidly kissed her closed eyes.

Far down the road, a neighbor was making his way back from the station. His voice could be heard singing the dirge of the Jews:

> "A man roams through the world,
> Going from city to city . . ."

Inside, the old men moaned: "O, Jerusalem, rent and dying, the tears of your children are as many as the waters of the sea. . . ."

fourteen
THE STORY OF MIRYAM

Miryam and Rogelio Miguez could understand each other only in song. Rogelio, the young Argentine, was the most talented singer in Entre Ríos. A finished improviser of the sad little songs, the *vidalitas,* he played and sang them very skillfully at the regional dances and brought tears to the eyes of the girls with the catch in his voice and the sighing of his illustrious guitar. He was an extraordinary young man. Very handsome, in a simple country way, he was outstanding among the young men, especially in the matter of affairs of the heart. No other young man could match the number of his. Rogelio, though, was not a pleasant youth. His face had the same quiet expression always, and he rarely smiled or laughed.

The other Gaucho helpers in the colony were envious of his good luck, and often mentioned his one great failing—his poor showing as a jackstones player. Rogelio had few friends among his fellow Argentines. On the other hand, the Jews of the colony esteemed him very highly as an excellent boy and a wonderful worker.

It seemed strange to no one that Jacobo Jalerman, his employer, should consider Rogelio something of a treasure. Don Jacobo, with his thin beard, sunken cheeks and beak nose, had been a student at the Hebrew school of Vilna, a teacher in Bessarabia, and was now a farmer in Entre Ríos. He loved to extol the excellencies of his helper, Rogelio. He talked at great length about the boy, bringing out endless examples of his worth. At one time, he convinced his fellow colonists that Rogelio would undoubtedly accept the Mosaic truths if his limited intelligence could only be made to understand their meanings.

"Do you remember that statement of Rabenu Yehuda?" he asked the teacher of the colony school. "The one in which he said that it was only a malevolent limitation of their brains that prevented all men from seeing the truth of Jehovah's law?"

His daughter, Miryam, did not argue the point. She needed no rabbinical interpretations of the Talmud to convince her that Rogelio was for her. She could not understand the young man's conversation—she had come from Russia only a short time ago, and the gaucho Spanish seemed as hard as a rock to crack—but she did understand his songs. When Rogelio sang one of his thrilling *vidalitas,* she would answer him with a Jewish song. The language was strange, but her singing delighted him. His face would blush with interest as he listened to this beautiful girl who was blonde as a light dusk, with the soft straw color of wheat.

When Rogelio and Don Jacobo went out to work in the fields, Miryam would bring them their breakfasts. They would all sit at the side of the last furrow and entertain each other in their individual tongues. The morning sun would warm them as Don Jacobo spoke of the plowing they had done that morning and of their oxen, who were so like the Biblical oxen—as big as mountains and as gentle as children. The oxen had names that recalled the Russia Don Jacobo had lived in: Czar, he called one. Moscow another. Czarevitch. . . .

"Alexander the Third has a sore on his neck," he said now.

"Don't worry about it, patron," Rogelio said. He turned to Miryam. "This is wonderful coffee, little mistress."

"Did you work hard this morning?"

"Not at all. We've just been playing . . ."

When Don Jacobo looked away, Rogelio would flick pebbles or grass at the girl with a smile.

The relations between these two began to cause talk in the colony. People were struck by the very liberal attitude of Miryam, who was, after all, the daughter of the very religious and well instructed Don Jacobo. From open comment, the talk soon developed into murmurs and insinuations. A boy, Isaac, had seen the couple sitting together on the bank of the stream, and Raquel, the Shochet's old mother, claimed to have seen them there and behind the house, as well.

Don Jacobo heard these things, but he made it plain that he did not believe them. When his friends of the synagogue made various hints, he answered with the same subtlety and always ended by saying: "Don't worry. Miryam won't marry a Christian. On the other hand, Rogelio is a young man who doesn't rob or kill. If you look in his room, you won't find any missing rolls of wire or the belts from a yoke." This last referred to an incident that had just occurred in the home of the colony's most devout family.

In spite of his feelings, Don Jacobo acted prudently—for he was a prudent person. He dismissed his helper, Rogelio, at the first pretext. The stories and gossip stopped. The Shochet himself announced one Sabbath that Don Jacobo was a man of honor and Miryam a very honorable girl—a girl who was Jewish to the core.

The matter ended in a very unexpected way.

Passover was being celebrated in the synagogue, the Shochet's ranchhouse. A large crowd of colonists attended, the girls in brightly colored dresses, the boys in riding habits. The early spring dusk was crowding the afternoon with night's first gloom and darkness, and the animals were beginning to grow restless in the nearby pastures. Don Jacobo, his sacred tunic over his shoulders, was explaining some complicated details of the Bible with his customary eloquence, when a child outside suddenly shouted: "Come! Come and see this! Look! Look!"

The colonists rushed out of the synagogue and witnessed this horrible scene: Mounted on his handsome sorrel, Rogelio came riding down the colony street at full gallop, with Miryam seated behind him. They passed the synagogue like the wind, the Gaucho proud and erect in the saddle, and she, with her loose hair flying staring defiantly at the people with burning eyes.

By the time the colonists had recovered from their surprise, the fugitive pair were a disappearing point in the distance. The last rays of the sun were touching up the dust they raised with spots of gold.

fifteen
THE HERDSMAN

Don Remigio Calamaco, herdsman for the colony of Rajíl, was a typical Gaucho. He was very old, but seldom out of the saddle. Riding in the pasture or along the edge of the fields, his whistles cut the air like sharp arrows. He was tall and broad, his wrinkled face cut by many scars; his hair was long, and so was his beard—the wind stirred it softly in the rhythm of the slow, steady gallop of his mare.

When still a youth, he had served under the great patriot, Crispín Velázquez, in the same company as the Commissary of Villaguay. On rainy afternoons, when the brooks ran like rivers, Don Remigio told tales of his past glory to the Jewish boys who sat with him around the *brasero* in his canvas tent. We would have a party then, for Don Remigio's servant girl would serve us tea and his son would sing songs of the Pampas to his own accompaniment on the battered guitar, the edge of which the old man often used for cutting his tobacco plug.

These were Don Remigio's favorite days. The animals were in the pasture; the colonists were home—they weren't working. Don Remigio would sit near the friendly brazier, fed by a piece of *quebracho* wood that gave off heat but not smoke. He told us of wonderful deeds. Sitting on the calfskin, with his injured leg stretched out—it had been permanently dislocated in a rodeo years ago—Don Remigio would roll one of his black tobacco cigarettes, put it in his mouth almost to the end, and begin to talk. His voice was hoarse, but it would rise and fall with emotion in his telling of interminable stories.

Don Remigio never failed to mention the name of the great soldier Crispín Velázquez, and if he noted any sign of doubt in his audience he would call on the absent but well-known Commissary, Don Benito Palas, as a witness. He had been Palas' sergeant years before, when robbers still roamed through the tall grass sections around San Gregorio.

Naturally, Don Remigio could not read. His learning consisted mostly of country aphorisms, of well remembered stories about long forgotten wars, of properly vulgar curses for clearing "traffic" james on the Las Moscas road, and sharp retorts and puns for shouting at his opponent—a cheat, of course, in a jackstones contest.

It went without saying, too, that so distinguished a Gaucho as Don Remigio was extremely skillful in the art of the *vidalita* and the dance. More than one countryman from Villaguay could still remember the triumphant victories that Don Remigio had scored in the regional feasts.

His dagger, too, was a terror to all. Its silver blade had reflected the moonlight in too many duels to remember.

He was an old man now, living in a leaky, windswept tent but Don Remigio could still evoke his exciting youth with a flourish. At those times, he would leave off his guerrilla war stories and take up a more familiar talent. He would exercise his thin skeletal fingers in the air as his fierce old face grew calmer and more reposed, and he called: "Bring me that guitar, Juan. I still know a little something."

He tuned the strings slowly and skillfully and then, after a long period of strumming rehearsal, moved into his musty and well-worn repertoire.

His songs were the old familiar *décimas* of the Gauchos—so called because they consisted of ten-line stanzas—songs that reflected the crude but pensive spirit of the Gaucho, that told of his valiant, barbarous spirit as well as the tenderness of his love.

"That's how they used to sing in my time," Don Remigio would say at the end of every *décima.*

Like all old people, Don Remigio, too, longed for the past—the time of Crispín Velázquez, when he had been young and brave. His tough old face took on a look of soft nostalgia when he remembered those days. A paladin with brave troops, he was ending his days in the ordinary, monotonous chores of a colony herdsman. Not even the rodeos of today were like the old ones—bursting with life and danger—and a man couldn't even indulge in a little bit of crime. The broad Pampas was divided into neat little farms now, bordered efficiently with wire fences, and his spirit that nurtured itself in the communism of the lawless past was oppressed by this new cut-and-dried order and peace.

His Gaucho friends were spread to all parts of Argentina, his comrades of the war dead and forgotten. He could look on these foreigners with only a bitter sadness as they plowed their measured fields in his wild country and carefully husbanded new calves and pullets.

Don Remigio's old age was as full of laments as his battered guitar; he seemed to carry the burdens of a conquered people. His life in Rajíl was a simple one: he broke and trained horses for the Jews and tempered the spirit of cows that refused to be milked. He could understand little of Jewish religion or ritual, but he admired the Jews for their spirit of work and their humility. He knew that a fire was never made on Saturday, and on Friday nights he would often go to the Shochet's or Mayor's house to work up the fire in the oven where the next day's meat and cakes were being cooked.

We all loved him; many of us wept the day we learned of his tragedy. That event climaxed his lief in a manner worthy of the soldier and the natural leader. It was typical of the original Gaucho, whose history, when it is told in future ballads, will shock the modern civilized generations.

No one of us in the colonies will ever forget that last act of Don Remigio's. Men still talk of it in the synagogue, and women are newly shocked when they hear of it.

It happened on a Sunday, near the little café, the Chapel, at the station. The *Gallegos*—Galicians from Spain who farmed the land north of the colonies—and the Jews were making their respectable purchases at the little grocery store. Outside, the Gauchos, in their usual holiday mood, were beginning to feel the drinks they'd had in the sun, and were setting up races and games. It was a clear, beautiful day. The nearby river, the Lizard, looked like a grey thread as it made its way past the miniature breakwater. Daisies spotted the green fields on either side of the river, and thistles spread a further stain of their own color.

Bets were made. Don Remigio slapped his boot with his whip and dared the young Gauchos. "You, Melitón! Let's see what that bay of yours can do! You're both as slow as a coachman's nag!"

As he hurled his whip about and flung out his arms, his thin poncho lifted and showed the silver-spotted belt holding the famed dagger and *boleadoras*. He took off his battered, high-crowned hat and slapped it against his thighs in excitement and mock anger; he stamped from one group of Gauchos to another, walking with stamping steps from group to group and from game to game. He would give a final decision in some argument or clarify some doubtful measurement in the game, reproaching, joking, or just humming as he stared at all with his fierce old eyes.

At times, Sergeant Rodríguez had to call out from his lookout in the doorway of the café to quiet some strident shouting in the discussions. The sergeant was in town with the Commissary, whose presence was required at the jackstones game.

Don Remigio, meanwhile, had gotten into a close, face-to-face argument with another Gaucho over the old man's asserting that his *pangare* could outrun any horse. Any horse!

"Juan!" Don Remigio shouted to his son. "Look, here! Show this fellow how that horse of mine can run!"

A bet was made. Juan mounted Don Remigio's horse; Castro, the Benítez Gaucho, was riding his sorrel. The Gauchos all moved over to the corral that would serve as finish line and grandstand for the race. From far off, the horses began their furious sprint, and the watchers could see how hard the two young Gauchos drove their mounts as they heard their shouts and calls over the sound of the rushing hoofbeats. Don Remigio's *pangare* was winning easily, and most of the Gauchos began to shout him on.

Coming up to the finish, the sorrel buckled and fell, throwing Castro to the ground. A heated argument followed. Castro shouted that if his horse hadn't fallen, they would easily have won the bet. Juan called him a fool and a liar, and the two jockeys, quiet and set now, faced each other to fight. As they crouched in preparation, old Don Remigio, rolling and lighting a cigarette, stood and watched calmly.

"Remember your honor, my son," he said in a quiet voice to Juan. "Stand up and fight well."

The struggle was brief. Their daggers flashed as the two young men crouched, leaped in and then locked arms, jockeying for position. The stamp of their feet and their quick breathing were the only sounds as they broke again and then dodged and plunged with barbaric Gaucho skill.

Castro was cold and sure in his attacks. Don Remigio's face darkened as his son began to move back. Castro was dominating the son—he was sure of his superiority. The old man was fingering his beard with his left hand, while his right gripped the handle of his dagger. His face was dark and angry now. His son, Juan, moved back in another attack and, jumping suddenly forward, Don Remigio plunged his own dagger into his son's neck at the back of his skull. "Don't retreat, coward! Don't retreat!" he shouted.

There was a moan from the boy, and the Gauchos moved back in horror. Slowly, Don Remigio turned and walked towards the café. Some Gauchos moved in and tried to lift the wounded boy with their trembling hands.

Castro had mounted his sorrel and was galloping off. The Gauchos began to whisper; there were murmurs of admiration for the old man who seemed a lone survivor of their loyal, hardy race—their people who had worked such wonders on these plains and who forgave all sins but cowardice. Bravery was the primary Gaucho trait; bravery was the race's chief nobility, the source of its true poetry.

And so this wonderful Gaucho and herdsman, Don Remigio Calamaco, ended his days and his deeds in a prison cell, wearied with age, with memories and with sorrows.

sixteen

THE DEATH OF REB SAUL

It happened in Rajíl. It was a pale wintry morning, and it was cold. The sun was coming up over the hills and tinting the frost that covered the ground. The fences, too, were frosted, as were the roofs of the ranchhouses and the roadway, and this little piece of Entre Ríos looked more like a village in the north, a little cut of the frozen Russian steppes dropped on the warm, friendly soil of the Gauchos.

It was the hour of the first chores. Reb Saul went back and forth from house to corral, preparing to take the team out to the far field. The kitchen of the house was filled with smoke of wood, and the children were huddled about the fire, gripping cups of *maté* and stamping their feet to keep warm. Goyo, the Gaucho worker, was trying to shake off sleep. He stretched and yawned and wrinkled his face. The old lady was searching through the hens' nests and voicing her usual complaint of the morning: "They never lay in the same spot."

"They're badly trained, *patrona*," Goyo said sleepily. He yawned.

The cry of the lapwings was heard from the pool, and from far off, where the grey line of the stream merged into the pale dawn, the mare could be heard whinnying in the quiet morning. Little by little, the sun rose high and reddened the clouds that moved like white stains along the metallic blue of the sky. There was movement and talk in all of the colony's houses now. Farmers and their helpers were hitching their oxen, still benumbed by the cold night. Oaths and exclamations could be heard from the neighboring corral, and the children called out advice as they laughed.

Ruth came into the kitchen, sleepy, her hair tousled. She had a woolen blanket wrapped around her fresh, robust beauty, giving her a look of primitive arrogance. She went up to the fire and poured herself a cup of *maté*. With a careless toss of her head, she dismissed a compliment from Goyo: "Don't say such foolish things. It's too early in the morning."

Standing near the door, Reb Saul began to pray. He slowly entwined his arm in the straps of one phylactery, the small leather box containing Scriptural passages, placed the other at his forehead and stood at the doorway. The white tunic gave his figure a priestly and Oriental look as he began the prayers. With typical sincerity he murmured the language that Jehovah used in speaking to his prophets. Reb Saul asked happiness for his own and a blessing for all the world's people.

As he finished, the sun was high and shining. The frost was melting and the paradise trees and shrubs seemed to come alive in the warming air of the morning. A slight breeze stirred the skeletal stumps of the plants in the bare garden, and the frogs began to pitch their dissonance against the brightening songs of the birds.

Reb Saul urged the Gaucho and the children on. The boys went to saddle the horses and the Gaucho went to the corral.

"Yoke up Fat and the Gentle One," Reb Saul said to him.

Don Goyo shrugged his shoulders and began to shout calls and orders to the beasts. They stared at him, then kicked at the frozen dung under their feet. Don Goyo leaned against the fence and smoked a cigarette. Then he took some time to tie the two oxen to the fence, although this seemed hardly necessary—they were so gentle and took the yoke easily.

Don Goyo was like that. He was very active in only one place—at the dinnertable, where he reached eagerly for food and held out his cup for *maté*. Since Reb Saul knew him well, he came into the corral now to urge him to get on with the yoking. "If we don't hurry," he said, "we won't even be able to make four rows of plowing."

The Gaucho did not answer him. He walked over towards the wall, calmly took down the yoke and placed it on one of the ox's neck.

"Not that one, Don Goyo," Reb Saul said. "Yoke up the Gentle One and Fat—this Chico worked all week and he's not feeling too well. I can see it."

"Listen, *patrón*, I don't like the Gentle One," the Gaucho said. "he steps out of the row too much."

Reb Saul tried to argue. He spoke very little Spanish, but he spoke energetically. Meanwhile, he kept smiling so that Gaucho would not take offence at his vehemence.

Don Goyo went on yoking Chico as if he had not heard.

Reb Saul was furious now. He pushed Goyo away and lifted the yoke from Chico's neck. The Gaucho's eyes turned bright with anger, and what happened then happened instantly. Reb Saul saw him, but the Gaucho already had his knife out, and when the old man lifted the yoke to defend himself, Goyo pushed it aside with his left hand and, jumping forward, drove his knife deep into the old man's chest.

Don Goyo walked out of the corral as if nothing had happened, and moved quietly towards the other houses. He was soon out of sight. When the boys came up with the horses, they found the old man's body between the still gentle oxen. The neighbors rushed up at their shouts and cries. The women burst into long loud lamentations immediately.

They lifted Reb Saul and carried his body into the ranchhouse, placing him tenderly on the floor in the center of the big room. Then they wrapped a white sheet around his body. His face was twisted in a look of pain, his eyes were open and sunken, and his full white beard stirred ever so slightly at the vibrating steps of those who came and went in the room. With his long hair, his full beard and his white tunic, Reb Saul resembled the figure of one of our great prophets.

seventeen

THE OWL

Jacobo was loping past Reiner's house on his prize pony when he saw the mother and daughter sitting on the steps and staring down the road. He greeted them in *criollo*, the gaucho form of Spanish. The old lady answered him in Yiddish and the girl asked if he had seen her brother Moisés, who had gone to the plains this morning to hunt thrush.

"Moisés?" Jacobo asked. "Was he on the white horse?"

"Yes."

"Did he go by way of Las Moscas?"

"No," the girl, Perla, said, "he took the San Miguel road."

"I haven't seen him then. I wasn't near San Miguel."

The old lady spoke, after a moment. Her voice showed worry and fear: "My son is late now. He's very late—and he only has some traps with him. He didn't take his revolver."

"That shouldn't worry you, Señora," Jacobo said quickly. "There's no danger in that section of the plains. You can ride all around there for days without meeting a soul."

"May God hear you!" Doña Eva said. "They were telling us the other day that bandits had been seen in one of Ornstein's fields. As close as that."

"No," Jacobo said. He shook his head and tried to reassure the old lady. There were no bandits where Moisés had gone. He, Jacobo, knew. He knew those places. He spurred the pony and turned in a wide arc so that Perla could see the full, thrilling picture of his horsemanship. As he galloped away, he waved to the two women who sat and watched him silently.

The sun was going down now; the autumn afternoon slipped towards the first vague haziness of night. The last rays of the sun were fringes of red on the far sky and magenta yellow on the nearer trees. With the pale green of the pasture grass, the yellow hue lent a sweet melancholy to the scene facing the women, and the old lady remembered an old Hebraic poem of a lone shepherdess leading home her sleepy flock of sheep under Canaan's sky.

The other houses of the colony were sinking into dusk, clinging to the last of the day with some random reflections of sunlight on their windows and the copper drains.

"It's late, my child," Eva said, "and Moisés isn't coming."

"Don't worry, mother. This isn't the first time he's been late. Remember last year, on Passover Eve, when he took the cart to the forest in San Gregorio. He came back with the wood the next day."

"Yes, I remember. But he had his revolver with him, and besides—there's a colony near San Gregorio."

The girl said nothing, and a long depressing silence followed. The crickets and frogs began to chirp and croak at the first signs of darkness. In the ponds the lapwings sounded and other flutterings could be heard from the nearest trees in the orchard.

An owl flew over the corral, hooted mournfully, and settled down on one of the post tops.

"That fellow's ugly, isn't he," the girl said.

The owl hooted again and stared at the two women. His eyes seemed to carry forebodings of evil.

"They say he's a bad omen."

"That's what they say," the other said, "but I don't believe it. What do country people know about such things?"

"But don't we Jews claim that the crow is a sign of death?"

"That's different."

The owl flew straight and low along the ground to the eave of their house. He stopped and hooted there, and then returned to his place on the post, continuing to stare at the two women.

From the dark shadows of the road, they heard the sounds of a horse galloping. The girl strained forward to see. She shook her head and settled back beside her tense mother. "It isn't white," she said. "It's a sorrel horse coming."

The beginnings of the evening breeze lifted phrases of a song from a neighboring house. It was a chant, one of those monotonous and lamenting chants, in which the writer uses popular jargon to mourn the loss of Jerusalem and to exhort the daughters of the "singular and magnificent" Zion to weep in the night so that their tears might awaken the pity of Jehovah. Without thinking, Perla began to sing in a low voice: *"Weep and moan, you daughters of Zion . . ."*

Later, in a more confident voice, she sang the couplet of the Spanish Jews that her teacher, Don David Ben-Azan, had taught her in school:

> *"We have lost Zion;*
> *Toledo, we have lost:*
> *Our tears are endless."*

Then, when her mother remained tense and quiet, the girl went back to the subject of omens in an effort to distract her. "Do you believe in dreams?" she said. "A few days ago, Doña Raquel told us about one that really frightened us."

After Perla had told the dream, her mother told her a "frightening" story of her own. A cousin of hers—who was as beautiful as a star—was betrothed to a boy in her village. He was a carter—very poor, very honorable, and very fearful of God—but the girl could not love him because he was hunchbacked. On the night of the betrothal, the wife of the Rabbi, who was a very saintly woman, saw a crow.

The fiancé sold one of his horses and bought a beautiful copy of *Siddur*, a prayerbook, which he presented as a gift to his betrothed. Two days before the wedding, the betrothal was annulled, and the following year the girl married one of the richest men of the village.

Remembering these long-past events made a deep impression on Doña Eva. As she sat with her daughter in the shadows, her face grew sadder still, and she went on to tell of miraculous happenings in a lower voice: The girl was married, yet happiness wasn't hers; almost as soon as they were born, her children died. All of them. And her fiancé? He had died.

The Rabbi in the city was consulted by the family and he agreed to study the case. He read through the Holy Scriptures and found a similar happening. He advised the woman to return the beautiful prayerbook to her dead betrothed. Then, she would find peace and happiness.

"Carry it with you tomorrow night," he told her, "under your right arm—and return it to him."

The poor woman did not say anything. The next night, as the moon came up, she left the house with the prayerbook under her arm. An unusual light rain was falling, prickling her face, and her feet were so unsteady with fear that they slipped about on the hardened snow. She reached the outskirts of the town, so tired and numbed she had to stop to lean against a wall. She thought of her dead children and of her first betrothed—his memory had been wiped out by the passage of so many eventful years. Now, as she leaned against the wall, she opened the prayerbook and stared at the beautiful, archaic printing of the pages. She had enjoyed looking through the book during feast days in the synagogue. Suddenly, her eyes dimmed, and as she blinked and looked up she saw the carter standing in front of her, his face shy but calm, his body bent and hunchbacked.

"This is your prayerbook, and I return it to you," she said to him.

The apparition—there was earth in his eyes and hair—put out a bony hand and received the book.

The girl remembered the further advice of the Rabbi and said: "Peace be with you, and please pray for me. I will ask God for your salvation."

The girl, Perla, sighed. As her mother had told this story, the night had closed in on them, but it was peaceful and a transparent night. In the distance, the fireflies blinked off and on like flying sparks, and reminded the old woman and the girl of the phantoms they had talked about. On the nearby fence the owl sat and stared at them, his brilliant eyes set and fixed like a statue's.

The girl, Perla, could not forget the phantoms and spirits. "You know, Mama, if the Gaucho believes such things about this bird, it may be that . . ."

Doña Eva looked over at the bird and then stared down into the black darkness of the road. In a low voice that trembled some, she said: "It may be, my child. Yes, it may be . . ."

A chill seemed to shake her, and her daughter moved closer to the old woman. Perla, too, felt a tightening in her throat. They stared down into the blackness, as the sound of horses' hooves came from far away. They strained forward—to hear better, to see through the black night. Their breaths caught, and the minutes seemed to stretch through their hearts, like long thin pains.

The dogs in the neighborhood had begun to bark, but the women heard the gallop growing clear and louder through the noise. Then, they saw the white horse break out of the blackness in a furious gallop. The mother and daughter jumped in their fright; their screams started as cries, then rose to a single strident moan. The sweating horse had slowed to a trot, and then stopped at the patio gate. He was riderless, and his saddle was covered with drying blood.

eighteen

CAMACHO'S* WEDDING FEAST

For two weeks now, the people of the entire district had been expectantly waiting for Pascual Liske's wedding day. Pascual was the *rich* Liske's son. The family lived in Espindola and, naturally enough, the respectable people of the colonies were looking forward to the ceremony and feast. To judge by the early signs, the feast was to be exceptional. It was well known in Rajíl that the groom's family had purchased eight demijohns of wine, a barrel of beer and numerous bottles of soft drinks. Kelner's wife had discovered this when she happened to come on the Liske's cart, stopped near the breakwater. The reins had broken, and the Liske's hired man was working frantically to replace them.

"The soft drinks were *rose* colored," she told the neighbors. "Yes!"

* Camacho is the name of a character in *Don Quixote* who suffers the same fate as the bridegroom in this story (translator's note).

she said, looking directly at the doubting Shochet's wife. "Yes, they were rose colored, and each bottle had a waxen seal on it."

Everyone agreed old man Liske's fortune could stand that kind of spending. In addition to the original land and oxen that he'd gotten from the Administration, Liske had many cows and horses. Last year's harvest alone had brought him thousands of pesos, and he could well afford to marry off his son in style without touching his principal.

Everyone further agreed that the bride deserved this kind of a wedding. Raquel was one of the most beautiful girls in the district, if not in the whole world. She was tall, with straw blond hair so fine and full it suggested mist; her eyes were so blue they made one's breath catch. She was tall and lithe, but her simple print dresses showed the full curving loveliness of a beautiful body. An air of shyness and a certain peevishness became her because they seemed to protect her loveliness.

Many of the colonists had tried to win her—the haughty young clerk of the Administration as well as all the young men in Villguay and thereabouts—but none had achieved a sympathetic response. Pascual Liske had been the most persistent of these suitors, but certainly not the most favored, at first. In spite of his perseverance and his gifts, Raquel did not like him. She felt depressed and bored because Pascual never spoke of anything but seedings, livestock and harvests. The only young man she had seemed to favor was a young admirer from the San Gregorio colony. She had gone out dancing with him during the many times he used to come to visit.

Her family had insisted she accept Pascual and the marriage had been arranged.

On the day of the feast, the invited families had gathered at the breakwater before Espíndola. A long line of carts, crowded with men and women, was pointed towards the colony. It was a spring afternoon, and the flowering country looked beautiful in the lowering rays of the sun. Young men rode up and down the line on their spirited

ponies, calling and signaling to the girls when the mothers were looking elsewhere. In their efforts to catch a girl's eye, they set their ponies
to capering in true Gaucho style. In their eagerness, some even proposed races and other contests.

Russian and Jewish songs were being sung in all parts of the caravan, the voices fresh and happy. At other points, the songs of this,
their new country could be heard being sung in a language that few
understood.

few speak Spanish

At last, the caravan moved into the village. The long line of heavy
carts, being gently pulled by the oxen, had the look of a primitive
procession. The carts stopped at different houses, and the visitors went
inside to finish their preparations. Then, at the appointed time, all
the invited guests came out together and began to make their way to
the groom's house.

Arriving at Liske's, they found that rumors of the fabulous preparation had not been exaggerated. A wide pavilion stood facing the
house with decorative lanterns hanging inside on high poles, masked
by flowered branches. Under the canvas roof were long tables covered with white cloths and countless covered dishes and bowls that
the flies buzzed about hopelessly. Old Liske wore his black velvet frock
coat—a relic of his prosperous years in Bessarabia—as well as a newly
added silk scarf of yellow, streaked with blue. With hands in his pock-
ets, he moved from group to group, being consciously pleasant to everyone and speaking quite freely of the ostentation and unusual luxury
of the feast. To minimize the importance of it all, he would mention
the price, in a lowered voice, and then, as if to explain his part in this
madness, would shrug his shoulders, saying, "After all, he's my only son."

The Hebrew word, *beniujid,* the only son, expresses this sentiment
very well, and it was heard frequently as many guests expressed their
praises of the fat Pascual. Even his bumpkin qualities were cited as
assets in the extraordinary rash of praise.

His mother was dressed in a showy frock with winged sleeves, and wore a green kerchief spread over her full shoulders. Moving quickly, in spite of her ample roundness, she went from place to place, talking and nodding to everyone in the growing crowd that was soon becoming as big and fantastic as the fiesta.

Under the side eave of the house, a huge caldron filled with chickens simmered over a fire, while at the side, in the deeper shadow, hung a row of dripping roasted geese. In front of these were trays with traditional stuffed fish stacked for cooling. What the guests admired more than the chicken-filled caldron, the roast geese, stuffed fish, and the calf's ribs that the cooks were preparing were the demijohns of wine, the huge cask of beer and, above all else, the bottles of soft drinks whose roseate color the sun played on. Yes, it was so. Just as they'd heard in Rajil, there were the bottles of rose-colored soft drinks with red seals on the bottles.

The music was supplied by an accordion and guitar, and the two musicians were already essaying some popular Jewish pieces. Voices in the crowd were tentatively humming along with them.

The bride was preparing for the ceremony in the house next to Liske's. Friends were dressing her, and her crown of sugar was already well smudged from constant rearrangement. Raquel was very sad. No matter how much the other girls reminded her of her wonderful luck—to marry a man like Pascual wasn't something that happened every day—she remained depressed. She was silent most of the time, and answered with sighs or short nods. She was a normally shy girl, but today she seemed truly sad. Those eyes that were usually so wide and clear now seemed as clouded as her forehead.

In talking about the guests, someone told Raquel that Gabriel had come with other people from San Gregorio. She grew more depressed at hearing his name and, as she put on the bridal veil, two big tears ran down her cheeks and fell on her satin blouse.

Everyone knew the cause of her weeping. Raquel and Gabriel had come to an understanding months ago, and Jacobo—that wily little know-it-all—had claimed he saw them kissing in the shadow of a paradise tree on the eve of the Day of Atonement. . . .

Pascual's mother finally arrived at the bride's house and, in accordance with custom, congratulated the bride and kissed her noisily. Her voice screeched as she called to let the ceremony begin.

Raquel said nothing. She shrugged in despair and stood hopelessly while the group of friends gathered at her back and picked up her lace-bordered train. The future father-in-law arrived with the Rabbi and the procession started.

Outside Liske's house, the guests were gathered about the tables, while inside the house Pascual, who was dressed in black, waited with friends and the father of the bride. When they heard the handclapping outside, they went out to the grounds and the ceremony began.

Pascual walked over to the canopy held up by couples of young men and women, and stood under it. He was joined immediately by his betrothed, who came escorted by the two sponsors. Rabbi Nisen began the blessings, and offered the ritual cup to the bride and groom. Then the bride began her seven turns around the man, accompanied by the sponsors. As she finished, an old lady called out that there had only been six, and another turn was made. The Rabbi read the marriage contract, that conformed entirely with the sacred laws of Israel. He sang the nuptial prayers again. The ceremony ended with the symbolic breaking of the cup. An old man placed it on the ground, and Pascual stepped on it with force enough to break a rock.

The crowd pressed in to congratulate the couple. Her friends gathered around the bride, embracing and kissing her, but Raquel was still depressed. She accepted the congratulations and good wishes in silence. Other guests gathered around the long table and began to toast and drink.

Old Liske proposed some dancing before they sat down to supper, and he himself began by moving into the first steps of the characteristic Jewish piece, "the happy dance," to the accompaniment of the accordion and guitar. At the head of the long table, the bride and groom stood together and watched the growing bustle without saying a word to each other. Facing them, standing very erect and pale, was Gabriel.

The guests called for the bride and groom to dance. Pascual frowned anxiously and shook his head. He did not dance. The calls and applause receded, and everyone stood waiting in embarrassment. Gabriel stepped forward suddenly and offered his arm to the bride. The accordion and guitar began a popular Jewish polka.

Gabriel tried to outdo himself, and he was a superb dancer. At one point he said something to Raquel, and she looked at him in surprise and grew still paler. People were beginning to whisper and move away. Israel Kelner had taken the arm of the Shochet as they both stepped away from the watching circle.

"Gabriel shouldn't have done this," Kelner said. "Everybody knows that he's in love with Raquel, and that she's *not* in love with her husband."

The Shochet pulled at his beard and smiled. "I don't want to offend anyone," he said. "I'm a friend of Liske's and he's a religious man—but Pascual is a beast. Did you see how mixed up he got when he was repeating the *hare-iad* pledge during the ceremony? Believe me, Rabbi Israel, I feel sorry for the girl. She's so beautiful and fine. . . ."

Little Jacobo took Rebecca aside and talked to her in Argentine *criollo*—he was the most gaucho of the Jews, as demonstrated now by his complete gaucho dress. "Listen, *negrita*," he began. "Something's going to happen here."

"A fight?" Rebecca whispered with interest.

"Just what I'm telling you. I was in San Gregorio this morning. Met Gabriel there. He asked me if I was going to the wedding—this one, of course. I said yes, I was, and he asked me about doing something later. . . ."

"A race?" Rebecca interrupted. "You mean to say that you made a bet with Gabriel? Oh, you men! And they said that he was heart-broken!"

"Oh, well," Jacobo said. He shrugged his shoulders. "As they say: Men run to races."

As night began to fall, the paper lanterns were lit, and many guests walked off a distance to see the effect of the lights. It was a special privilege of the rich to have such lights, and the last time they'd been seen here was during the visit of Colonel Goldschmith, a representative of the European Jewish Committee.

The next item was dinner, a banquet that bars description. The guests were seated and the bride and groom served the "golden broth," the consecrative dish of the newlyweds. Then the platters of chicken, duck and fish began to circulate; and the wine was poured to a complete and unanimous chorus of praise directed to the hostess.

"I've never eaten such tasty stuffed fish."

"Where could you ever get such roast geese as this?" the Shochet asked.

Rabbi Moisés Ornstein delivered the eulogy and added: "I must say that no one cooks as well as Madam Liske. Whoever tastes her dishes knows that they are a superior person's."

Fritters of meat and rice, wrapped in vine leaves, were served next, while more beer and wine quickened the spirits of the guests.

The bride excused herself, saying that she had to change her dress. She left the party accompanied by her friends. Her mother-in-law had started to go with them, but Jacobo stopped her. "Madam Liske!" he said. "Sit down and listen to your praises. Sit down and hear what we think of this wonderful banquet. We'll be made if you leave," he said, when she seemed reluctant to stop. "We're enjoying ourselves very much and we want to share this with you."

"Let me go, my boy," she said. "I have to help my daughter-in-law."

"Rebecca will help her. Sit down. Sit down. Rebecca!" Jacobo turned to shout. "Go and help the bride!"

The old lady sat down—everyone about had joined in the urging—and Jacobo brought her a glass of wine so that they could drink a toast.

"When one has a son like yours," the Shochet said to Madam Liske, "one should be glad."

The toasts were offered and drunk, and this clinking of glasses, lusty singing and music could be heard over all the grounds. The sky was full of stars, the atmosphere lightly tinged with clover and the scent of hay. In the nearby pasture, the cows mooed and the light wind stirred the leaves.

Jacobo got up and excused himself. "I have to see about my pony," he explained. "I think he might need a blanket."

"I'll look after my mare," Gabriel said, as he stood up to go with him.

They moved away from the group, and Jacobo took Gabriel's arm: "Listen, the bay is saddled and waiting by the palisade," he said. "The *boyero's* kid is watching him and the gate is open. At the first turn there's a sulky all set. The Lame One is watching there. Tell me, have you got a gun?"

Gabriel did not seem to hear this last point. He patted Jacobo's arm and started to walk towards the palisade. After a few steps, he turned to look back. "And how will Raquel get away from the girls in there?"

"Don't worry about that. Rebecca's there."

When the girls who were with the bride did return to the party, Madam Liske asked for her daughter-in-law. "She's coming right away with Rebecca," they told her. Then Rebecca returned alone, and gave the old lady still another excuse. Jacobo was doing his best to distract Madam Liske with toasts. Others took it up, and there was a great clinking of glasses and mumblings of toasts. The musicians continued to play and the guests to eat and drink. The jugs of wine were being refilled continuously, and no one's glass was ever low.

Pascual, the groom, looked fat and solemn and said nothing. From time to time, he would dart a quick look at the bride's empty chair. The gallop of a horse was heard at that moment, and then, soon after, the sounds of a sulky starting off.

Jacobo whispered into Rebecca's ear: "That's them, isn't it?"

"Yes," the girl whispered back, "they were leaving when I came away."

The continued absence of the bride was worrying her mother-in-law and, without saying anything, she slipped into the house to see. She came out immediately.

"Rebecca, have you seen Raquel?" she said.

"I left her in the house, Señora. Isn't she there?"

"She's not."

"That's funny . . ."

The old lady spoke to her husband and to her son, Pascual. The guests were beginning to whisper among themselves. That saw that something had gone wrong. The accordion and guitar went silent. The guests began to stand up; some glasses were tipped over, but no one paid any attention. A few of the guests moved towards the house. Others asked: "Is it the bride? Has something happened to the bride?"

The Shochet of Rajíl asked his friend and counterpart from Karmel about the point of sacred law if it was true that the bride had fled.

"Do you think she has?" the Shochet of Karmel asked.

"It's possible. Anything is possible in these situations."

"Well, I think that divorce would be the next step. The girl would be free, as would her husband. It's the common course."

Meanwhile, the excitement was growing all around them. Old Liske grabbed the Gaucho's little son. "Did you see anything out there? Out there on the road?" he said.

"Yes. Out there, on the road to San Gregorio. I saw a sulky, with Gabriel—he was driving it—and there was a girl sitting with him."

"He's kidnapped her!" Madam Liske screamed. Her voice was close to hysteria. "Kidnapped her!"

Shouts and quick talking started all over the grounds now. Most of the crowd were genuinely shocked and surprised. When old Liske turned to abuse the father of the Gaucho boy, the man stood up to him, and they were soon wrestling and rolling in the center of pushing and shouting guests. The table was overturned, and spilled wine and broken glass added to the excitement. The Shochet of Rajíl mounted a chair and shouted for order. What had happened was a disgrace, he said, a punishment from God, but fighting and shouting would not ease it any.

"She's an adulteress!" shouted the enraged Liske, as he sought to break out of restraining hands. "An infamous adulteress!"

"She is not!" the Shochet answered him. "She would be," he said, "if she had left her husband 'after one day, at least, after the marriage,' as our law so clearly says it. This is the law of God, you know, and there is no other way but that they be divorced. Pascual is a fine, honorable young man, but if she doesn't love him, she can't be made to live under his roof."

The Shochet went on in his usually eloquent and wise way, and he cited similar cases acknowledged by the most illustrious rabbis and scholars. In Jerusalem, the sacred capital, there had occurred a similar case, and Rabbi Hillel had declared in favor of the girl. At the end, the Shochet turned to Pascual: "In the name of our laws, Pascual, i ask that you grant a divorce to Raquel and that you declare, here and now, that you accept it for yourself."

Pascual scratched his head and looked sad. Then, in a tearful voice, he accepted the Shochet's proposal.

The crowd grew quiet and the guests soon began to leave, one by one, some murmuring, some hiding a smile.

Well, as you can see, my patient readers, there are fierce, arrogant Gauchos, wife-stealers and Camachos, as well as the most learned and honorable of rabbinical scholars in the little Jewish colony where I learned to love the Argentine sky and felt a part of is wonderful earth. This story I've told—with more detail than art—is a true one, just as I'm sure the original story of Camacho's feast is true. May I die this instant if I've dared to add the slightest bit of invention to the marvelous story.

I'd like very much to add some verses—as was done to the original Camacho story—but God has denied me talent. I gave you the tale in its purest truth, and if you want couplets, add them yourself in your most gracious style. Don't forget *my* name, however—just as our gracious master Don Miguel de Cervantes Saavedra remembered the name of Cide Hamete Benegeli and gave him all due credit for the original Camacho story.

And if the exact, accurate telling of this tale has pleased you, don't send me any golden doubloons—here, they don't even buy bread and water. Send me some golden drachmas of, if not, I'd appreciate a carafe of Jerusalem wine from the vineyards of my ancestors planted as they sang the praises of Jehovah.

May He grant you wealth and health, the gifts I ask for myself.

nineteen

A SOCIAL CALL

The big house of Don Estanislao Benítez stood a little outside Rajíl. Between the pasturelands and the station at Los Moscas, his acreage spread, cut into well-plowed fields or broadly stained with the red of maguey trees. On the highest point of his land, in a spot that enjoyed rare shade, the big-windowed mansion stood. Don Estanislao was one of the oldest Argentines of the region, a friend of Urquiza as well as a compatriot and comrade of the great Don Crispín.

Don Estanislao was a typical figure of his time. Heroic legends told of his bravery, and the courage and fire that had made him one of the most daring soldiers of his time now served to make this old man a fine rider and horsebreaker in the rodeos and fiestas.

Like Don Remigio Calamaco, the illustrious herdsman of Rajíl, Don Estanislao was noble and brave. There were two memories that added pride and prestige to his active old age. Seated at the head of the family table, or by the fireside, he would often refer to his greatest day as a soldier of Urquiza's: "When Don Bartolo came to confer with Urquiza and we had the big meeting at the Forks, Don Justo José Urquiza said to him, 'This is one of those that I spoke to you about,' and then Don Bartolo gave me his hand."

He would slowly raise his right hand for them to see—as if the pressure of that warm clasp could still be seen on its rough, knotty surface—and his eyes would cloud under the thick drooping eyebrows.

Then, he would turn to the subject of Juan Moreira, stories of whose adventures his daughter used to read him. The girl had been educated at a college in Villaguay.

"My comrade, Doctor Miguez, God rest his soul," the old man said, "he became a lawyer in Uruguay, you know—he read to me one day from a newspaper in Buenos Aires how Juan Moreira died."

These two facts gave him an incredible advantage over the other Gauchos. He was as good as bread; much respected and loved. A friend of the Jews in the colony, he visited Rajíl almost every day to help in the killing of the calves. He would lie on his poncho at the side of the corral, smoking a black cigarette and talking to the men. If there was trouble roping or tying up the animal, the old man mounted his horse, unloosed his *reata,* and in a few moments had the animal trussed and ready.

Don Estanislao invited the Shochet to his house, and Rabbi Abraham promised to visit him with his family. When the day came, the Shochet yoked his two gentle oxen to the cart and, with his wife and daughters, started for the mansion of La Lomada. Jacobo went along on his white mare.

A warm night was falling. The fields seemed to breathe softly under the clear, starry sky. The brook complained quietly as it moved down the pasture amide the timid bleating of sheep. The dogs barked at the white round moon reflected in the milky whiteness of the breakwater pond.

The Shochet's cart moved slowly. The black oxen pushed their foreheads against the yoke straps and walked with a quiet rhythm on the long shadow of Jacobo and his mare. On the other side, the skinny little dog *Dum* raced back and forth, his tail bristling, and rushed into the grass every once in a while to chase a partridge. Behind them, the black breakwater moved back into the shadows.

The travelers did not speak. Individually, they felt a secret, soothing emotion. The softness of the night was quieting—so, too, was the dark blue sky and the joy of living so close to a bountiful nature with one's heart and spirit open to her simple purity. A bell sounded from afar, the humble little bell of the chapel near Don Estanislao's. Then the Shochet remembered that it was a Christian feast day. The bell tolled again in the vague distance, its sound hardly perceptible, but the spirit of the Hebrew theologist, Don Abraham, filled as it was with the Talmud and thoughts of Jerusalem, was moved by the distant sound. A deep peace swept over him; his nerves quieted, his body relaxed in a pleasant, safe feeling of well-being. He pressed his wife to him—she, too, had gown young with the blessings of this new country. He kissed her tenderly on the cheek. "Praise be to God!" he murmured in a quiet voice.

But he would not go on with the idea that beat in his brain.

They stopped before the gate, and were immediately surrounded by a barking, surging mass of dogs. Without thinking it strange for a Jew, Jacobo shouted out the typical greeting of the Pampas: "Hail Mary! Ave María!"

One of Don Estanislao's young Gaucho helpers came rushing out and shooed off the dogs with slaps and kicks. He had recognized his friend Jacobo, and turned to shout back towards the house. "Master! You have visitors. It's Don Abraham and his family!"

The Shochet and the women got down from the cart. Don Estanislao came out and greeted them warmly, and his women folk gathered around the Shochet's wife and daughters with the customary hugs and kisses. The maid began to prepare the *maté* at once and they all sat down beneath the house's giant eaves. There was immediate laughter and talking, no one having thought it necessary to ask the visitors what was their country of origin or which was their race.

Rabbi Abraham was dignified, solemn and courteous. He nodded frequently to the friendly questions and comments without fully understanding their meanings. Jacobo was the one who did the talking. Playing with his heavy gaucho whip, he told about one incident on the journey, the snapping of a rein strap, and broke into his story with typical gaucho praise for the taste of the *maté* that was being served by Deolinda, Don Estanislao's oldest daughter.

"Not even in heaven do they taste the likes of this!" he said.

"How you flatter us!" Madam Benítez said. "How you do!" But she smiled coquettishly at the boy.

Don Estanislao was talking with his usual fluency, gesturing a good deal and jumping into his own words. The soft moonlight shone on this thin, bony figure, sharply silhouetting his silvery beard and rustic profile, Don Abraham's profile, too, seemed gaucho in its silhouette of long hair, its fine beard, beaked nose and high forehead. He was dressed in gaucho pantaloons with the broad sash about his waist.

As she served the *maté*, Deolinda moved back and forth from the kitchen. Her magnificent black hair fell to her shoulders in thick tresses, and her skirt rustled excitingly as she walked. Her big eyes were filled with fire and pleasure, and the clear, pure tone of her voice seemed to cut the air as she talked.

Don Abraham composed a hymn of praise for his friend's beautiful daughter. It was conceived in his usual elegance and erudition and, after a great effort, he succeeded in translating it into Spanish. "Don Estanislao," he said, "your nobility is reflected in the beauty of your daughter because, as one of our most venerated teachers has said, only the worthy can engender beauty."

Don Estanislao answered him—though he had not understood too well. "That's just how it is," he said.

The women had stared a conversation about domestic matters. Doña Gertrudis was enumerating the wonderful qualities of her cow, La Gordinflona. "She's as gentle as a child," she said. "I milk her twice a day. She gives a pail of milk in the morning and one in the afternoon. She never hides anything."

The Shochet's wife was astonished. She was very sorry, but she couldn't say the same about her cow—*there* was a sly, unruly creature!

Jacobo interrupted when he saw his mistress stumbling over her Spanish. "Yes! That cow. If we don't tie her to a post, and hold her too, we'd never get a drop out of her. After that, you have to watch her. She might kick over the pail."

The subject changed to hens and the number of eggs they gave. Doña Gertrudis complained about her cat, who had the habit of chasing the pullets.

"What a cat!" Deolinda said. "Yesterday he killed a nightingale of mine."

The conversation died slowly, as if the soft, quiet night was spreading its peaceful influence everywhere. The trees were in full bloom and spread their perfume over all. The daisies that were thickly spread over the orchard looked clean and white in the light of the bright moon.

"In all the world, there isn't a sky like this one," Don Abraham said.

He explained that he had been in Palestine, in Egypt and in Russia, but nowhere had he seen a sky as intensely blue as that of Entre Rios. "This sky is soft, yet protective," he went on. "If one finds oneself alone in the country here, one doesn't feel afraid. The sky is so reassuring, so loving."

The old Gaucho nodded. He understood Don Abraham perfectly. His pure simple soul was also relaxed in the warmth and security of this glorious night; beneath his incomparable native sky that offered protection, warmth and freedom. At that moment, they heard the bell of an ox tinkle softly near the corral and the pleasant homely sound lent a further reassurance.

The old Gaucho sighed deeply and felt himself nestling into the warm protective embrace of his native fields. He had been right, he thought, in risking his life for this land, in fighting so furiously—in bringing such fears to his enemies.

Yes. The old man reached back and took down his guitar from the wall. His thin fingers plucked tentatively at the strings and then, in a shaking voice, he began to play and sing an appropriate variation of the Pampas couplet:

> "Entre Ríos, land of mine!
> Where is there a sky like thine?
> Where are there hills and rivers . . ."

A cock crowed from afar, but the sound did not break the feeling.

twenty
WITCHES

"Do I believe in witches?" said Rabbi Abraham. "Well, my friend, that's a very important subject. Witchcraft! Now, let me see," and the Shochet began a long, rational speech regarding his opinions of this problem. "The Talmud says," he added in a very serious tone, "that there are two forces guiding the soul of each of us: the good angel and the evil spirit—the one that in ancient Hebrew was called Satan. So, you see, there's no possibility of denying it. The Talmud expressed the point very clearly. If angels exist, then devils must exist too, and if they do, they can induce unholy people to do their work."

The subject of witchcraft had come up because of a piece of news that had disturbed all the neighbors meeting in the synagogue that Sabbath. It seemed that Reb Ismael Rudman had heard strange noises on his roof at midnight. He paid no attention. "It's the wind," he thought.

But, a few minutes later, he heard the noise again. He knew it was not the wind now, because he went to the window and saw that the little percale curtain was not moving at all. Meanwhile, to judge by the noise, something odd was happening on the roof. Ismael decided to find out for certain. Climbing up to the edge, he could look over the whole roof of straw. From there, too, he could see the whole colony resting snugly and quietly in the warm, moonlit night. The animals were scattered but sleeping in the pastures and the little river looked like a white slit. The breakpier was a dark black mass, at his back.

There was nothing on the roof—he saw nothing there, and yet he heard his wife in the house saying that she still heard the noise. "There's nothing on the roof!" he shouted down to her.

Brane, his wife, was very alarmed. "Come down! Come down!" she said. "Who knows? It might be something evil . . ." and in a lowered voice she began to recite the prayer against phantoms. She was in a nightshirt, with her unbraided hair falling to her shoulders in straight, faded blonde strands; some stray wisps of it were shadowing the wrinkles on her unusually large forehead. The shirt had come open at the neck and her exhausted breasts took on the blue tones of moonlight. A vague terror gripped her soul and she felt a sudden chill spreading through her body.

"Ismael, come down!" she called again, in a voice that shocked and surprised him. "Come down."

Now, Ismael had rarely felt a fear of strange noises in the night and he was still very doubtful about this one, but when he heard the fright in Brane's voice, he too felt a sudden terror. He jumped down without a word.

They did not sleep anymore that night. With the window tightly closed and the door barred, they spent the remaining hours thinking over this strange phenomenon. Meanwhile, the noises on the roof continued. At Brane's insistence, Reb Ismael brought out the Siddur prayer book and read prayers that were especially fortuitous for dispelling malignant influences by invoking the name of the Most

Sacred. This time, however, the divine word had little effect. The noises continued, and Ismael and Brane felt a dark wind brush against the wall of their house, felt a tremor run through the roof . . .

A cock crowed in the yard, the moon grew dim, and absolute prevailed. The two fell asleep at dawn, and awoke very late. The morning was full, already.

"You must get to the synagogue," his wife said to Ismael.

"I will."

When he was dressed, Ismael opened the window. The light of a beautiful day filled the room. When he turned to look at his wife, Ismael stopped in terror. He could hardly reach the chair to sit down, and he kept breathing deeply of the fresh morning air in an effort to revive himself. One complete half of his wife's hair had turned grey!

"Extraordinary," the Shochet was saying, as they talked about it at the synagogue. "Most extraordinary."

"It is!" replied Kelner. "It is that!"

"It's witches," someone said in a tremulous voice.

"Nothing else!" another said. "It must be witches. Evil spirits!"

A discussion began about witches, ghosts and evil spirits.

Moisés Hintler thought that all such things were old wives' tales. He had always lived on the outskirts of his native city in Russia and he had never seen or heard anything like spirits or witches, and had never even heard tell of them. "I once spent a whole night in the middle of a forest," he said in a confident voice, "and didn't hear a thing. I slept so well . . ."

"I'm not bringing this up as a proof of anything," Kelner began. "You know I'm not superstitious, but . . ." He told of a curious happening. Of course, he said quickly, he hadn't been there to witness it. Nevertheless, it deserved the strongest credibility because he'd heard it from the lips of the Rabbi of Tulchin—such an honorable man wouldn't waste his time deluding a friend. After all, *there* was a true Rabbi! None could . . .

"As I was saying," Kelner went on, "this particular family from Haisin was making a long journey. At that time, coaches were used for these trips, and there was very little protection on the highways. These travelers were very fearful, and they held their hands on their pistols and commended their souls to God. Bandits were bold in those days, and they would often attack farmhouses and even villages—and carry away the wealth of the place as well as the girls.

"You can imagine how this family felt when after only a short time of traveling, they saw that the sky was growing dark and that the road they were on was approaching a dense forest. Fearfully, they asked the coachman if there was any danger in these parts.

"There always is," the Muscovite said. "There always is."

"The young men—there were three of them—gripped their pistols; the old many prepared the ammunition, and the women began to pray in low voices. Before long, the dark clouds had burst into pouring rain and the dark bitter night closed in on them. Just before they came to the forest, however, one of the young men noticed a light towards the right. He pointed it out to the coachman and the Muscovite turned up a small side-road towards the light. "It must be a tavern," he said.

"It looks like a tavern," the old man answered, trying to keep his voice calm.

When they arrived at the place, the young men called and then got out to bang on the door.

"There's a light, but they don't answer," said the coachman. "I won't go into that place."

"It's raining so hard, they may not hear," one of the young men said.

They continued to bang at the door and shout. Finally, a man appeared in the window at the side of the door. "Hey, there! How many are you?" he shouted.

"Eight!" one of the young men answered.

"Seven! Because I'm not going in," the coachman shouted.

The others entered the "tavern." It was a dirty, sordid place. The smoky light from thick tallow candles showed cracked walls, stained with soot, a heavy cross-beamed ceiling with thick cords hanging from some of the beams. With the door closed, the sound of the rain diminished, and in that moment the bodies and souls of the travelers froze with fear as a low, moaning cry, that seemed to come from the cellar, broke into the quiet. The men looked at each other.

"Can this be the Inn of the Tartars?" the youngest of the sons asked his father.

"It may be. . . ."

A long silence followed the cry. The Inn of the Tartars was a famous hideout where a band of raiders called "The Tartars" held their hostages until they were ransomed by relatives from the city. The travelers thought about this as they looked around the "tavern" and saw that all the doorways and windows had strong iron bars on the outside.

The old father was prudent. He saw that death was near and that it would be of little use to fight or cry. "Let us pray," he said, "and invoke the aid of our ancestors."

The rain increased, and the howling wind made the heavy beams of the ceiling creak as the thunder seemed to penetrate the very house. Hours passed.

Once, when they looked at the little window leading to the other parts of the tavern, they saw the terrible face of the man who had opened the door staring in at them. He moved quickly away. Moments later, they heard the roll of a grindstone and the sound of knives being sharpened.

They all began to pray in low voices, beating their breasts.

"God will protect us," the old man affirmed.

"Hear us, God!" his wife said. "I promise to burn fine candles for a year before the sanctuary in the synagogue."

The knocker on the door sounded suddenly.

"People are coming," the old man said.

"Can it be the bandits?"

"Don't talk foolishly," he said to his wife. "They're our saviors."

The "Tartars" would not open the door. Loud claps of the knocker sounded, and new bursts of thunder filled the travelers with new fears.

Finally, the door was opened and a crowd of people came in. "This way," the tavern keeper said rudely, trying to lead them past the room where the travelers were, "this way! That room's closed."

The new arrivals ignored him, however, took the chain off the door and came into the room. They were a group of men and women, obviously ladies and gentlemen, who were dressed in bright holiday clothes. The old man went up to them.

"I thank God that he heard our prayers."

"It's pouring outside, but none of you are wet," one of his daughters said, as she stared at the new people.

"You mustn't wonder about such things, my child," the old man said to her.

One of the new arrivals had only one arm. He went up to the door and banged it hard with his good first to call the owner. The man appeared immediately.

"Bring us something to eat and drink," said the one-armed man. "Good meat and good wine!"

"The cellars are empty," the owner told him.

"I'll go with you to see." He pushed the owner forward and followed him out. A few minutes later, the one-armed man returned with all the people who had been held captive in the cellar. The travelers and the costumed people greeted them happily and everybody started to laugh and sing. Meanwhile, the storm outside had abated and the moon had appeared.

The people left the tavern, and the travelers, together with those that had been rescued from the cellar, took up their journey to Haisin in the coaches. Behind them came their rescuers, in coaches that were as festively bedecked as the costumes they wore.

Toward dawn, when some of the travelers happened to look back, they saw that the festive coaches and their rescuers had vanished into mist, and, far back, they saw that the Inn of the Tartars was burning with bright, high flames.

"Yes," Kelner finished, "The Rabbi of Tulchin, a very learned and truthful man, told me of this happening. He knew of it because that same old man whose family had been saved had come to him to ask about giving thanks for their salvation. The Rabbi of Tulchin knew who those rescuers were—the ones that had vanished into the mist. He knew!"

"And how about the story of the cross in Las Moscas?" Young Jacobo was anxious to keep these ghost stories going.

This particular one was an old story in the community. One day, a man from Karmel had come looking for the house of Don Estanislao Benítez. Passing through Rajíl, he asked one of the Gauchos for directions to the rancher's house.

"It's very simple, sir," the Gaucho said. "Go straight until you come to the breakwater, turn left and walk a little ways until you see a cross, turn right then, and a half league from there is Don Estanislao's."

The man followed the Gaucho's directions, saw the cross, and arrived quickly at Don Estanislao's.

On another day, a second traveler asked directions to Don Estanislao's from the same Gaucho, but got lost when he tried to follow them out. He returned to Rajíl when it was very late and said that he hadn't seen any cross at all. The next day the Gaucho accompanied him to the place where one turned right after seeing the cross. The Gaucho pointed it out to him. It was a half kilometer away.

"Don't you see the cross there?" he said.

"No, I don't," the traveler said.

"Right there, man. Between those trees!"

The traveler stared. Finally, he said, "Yes, I see it. I see it now."

This same business of not seeing the cross and then having it pointed out happened many times. When Don Estanislao heard about it, he went to the spot to investigate and saw that no cross had ever been there.

"I don't believe it," the Gaucho said. "I've been passing by that spot for ten years. I ought to know." He went to the place again and studied the spot. "Someone took the cross away," he said, "and covered up the ground."

When another Gaucho's wife head about these investigations, she said: "Don't they know about the cross of Las Moscas? The witches put it there and then take it away. I've seen it there."

From that time on, many people feared going too near Las Moscas, and some said they had actually seen the witches moving about there.

"It was probably witches," someone said now, "who robbed the yoke and straps from the Mayor and those clothes from Hintler's house."

Another laughed: "It was the only thing we needed to complete our colony. Now, we even have witches to rob straps and ropes."

"And to frighten the Rudmans."

But the case of the Rudmans was not funny. After prayers the neighbors went to look over the house. Reb Ismael Rudman was with them. They examined the roof of the poor little house carefully. Then they went inside, Ismael and the Shochet leading the way. As they came up to the bed in the corner, they let out a shout. Ismael's wife, Brane, lay dead on the floor, her mouth twisted in a grimace of fear.

twenty one
DIVORCE

"Give us your opinion of the case, Reb Jonas."

"I think it would be better if Rabbi Abraham did. As the Shochet, he understands the laws and the true concept of justice."

The Shochet thought otherwise: "I think it would be better if the old men gave their opinions first."

This scene was taking place in Israel Kelner's house. The oldest of the villagers were meeting there to pass judgment on a plea for divorce. Being the first in the colony's history, it had aroused a good deal of feeling and interest. None of the old men was missing from this meeting, and seated near the window, in the center of the group, was the thin, imposing figure of the Moroccan Jew, Moisés Urquijo de Albinoim. He was in the colony to visit his son, a teacher at the local school, and being so learned in the sacred literature, he had been invited to the discussion. He spoke classical Hebrew, and expressed himself slowly and carefully.

Reb Israel bowed respectfully to Don Moisés and said: "Our guest should give his opinion first."

Fingering his long full beard, Don Moisés Urquijo de Albinoim asked that he be given the details of the case. The men all sat down around the table of cracked, broken boards, that was covered with the Sabbath cloth, and began to tell him the details. Meanwhile, the young Gaucho helper of the house served the *maté,* and the hostess was praised for the tea and cake she herself served.

"The representatives of the husband and wife are here," Kelner explained. "Reb Malaquías is speaking for the husband, and Reb Joel for the wife. The couple has been married for three years now. They live near San Antonio and are very honorable people."

Speaking for the husband, Reb Malaquías interrupted: "Reb Simón doesn't want a divorce."

The wife's representative, Reb Joel, said: "Let us put down the statements of the parties, have them established by the Shochet according to law, and then we and the witnesses will sign. The wife insists on a divorce," he finished.

Don Moisés Urquijo de Albinoim, a man who knew all details of the sacred literature, asked permission to question the representatives. He obtained this permission, and with the utmost courtesy he began: "The very honorable Reb Malaquías will tell us now if, in the name of Reb Simón, he accuses the wife before these judges."

"I do not accuse her," the Reb said.

"And you, Reb Joel, do you accuse the husband in the wife's name?"

"I do not."

Don Moisés stood up. "We see, my very respectable friends, that sin is not the cause of this petition for divorce—and we should thank God for that. We should praise the Most High for His wisdom in not permitting His good children—ourselves, the Jews—to be led into sin. Now, this case, my very wise friends, is one that requires thought and meditation. I hope, first, that Rabbi Abraham will enlighten us on what the law says about such a case. These two who are involved are honorable persons, and the cause of the divorce is not adultery, which the sacred texts condemn. The divorce is asked because of what Hillel—may his memory be blessed!—refers to in his very just pronouncements as 'little everyday things.' I say that we should not separate this couple."

"I won't vote for the divorce," Kelner said.

"I won't sign the papers," the Shochet added.

"We won't grant the separation," others said.

Don Moisés then invited the representatives of the couple to give their opinions. He did this very respectfully. Reb Joel was well versed in theology. He turned in his chair, took a swallow of water, and gave the following opinion:

"The wife is a virtuous woman. She knows how to respect her husband, how to keep his house well and how to attend to all wifely duties. But, she doesn't love her husband. She married him under pressure of her parents, as the saying goes, and, as our Books always predict, this is a sad and deplorable lack and makes the marriage a very difficult one. Not to like or love a husband means that the wife is condemned to pain and has no pleasure whatsoever. Let us remember the precepts offered in the Book of the Talmud that deals with matrimony—those precepts that have been so admired by the wisest rabbis. In the book Muschim, the Talmud says: 'Should a wife, for any reason, stop loving her husband, she must separate from him and not accept his caresses, for a child born of such union would suffer the consequences of the absence of love.' And so, in the name of the Sacred Law, I ask you, most respectful of judges, to grant this divorce."

"Reb Joel," said Don Moisés, "we have listened to you with feelings of satisfaction. You have been very eloquent, but now let us listen to Reb Malaquías."

"I have nothing to say," Malaquías replied. "Reb Simón loves his wife and considers her perfection itself. Nevertheless he is prepared to grant the divorce because the unhappy man knows that his wife cannot stand him. He doesn't want to cause her any more affliction; besides, his own life is plagued by constant misery. How can one live under the same roof with a woman who doesn't respect one? Since I understand all this, I join with Reb Joel in asking for the divorce. It is a just petition."

The Shochet suggested that they begin deliberation of the case. Then, while the old men discussed Talmudic statements and clauses in their grave, solemn way—acting as a Sanhedrin council in the middle of the Argentine countryside—the little Gaucho helper made frequent trips with the *maté*, a drink proving more popular than its counterpart, European tea. The old men were unacquainted with Argentine law, but they applied the laws of the Kingdom of Israel and so brought the wisdom and jurisprudence of Hillel, Gamaliel and Ghedalia to the Argentine pampas. Present, too, was a representative of the Talmudists of the Golden Age in Spain, Don Moisés Urquijo de Albinoim, looking very dignified and stately, speaking a cultured tongue and reflecting the mature sense of a disciplined yet rare spirit.

He was pompous, yet subtle, and here, in this small, clay-walled ranchhouse, he recalled the thoughts and reasonings of the great medieval Hebraists of Toledo and Córdoba, and revived once more the rich and profound ideas of the great Jews who had continued the traditional culture of Jerusalem under the Castilian rulers.

On the parchment the Shochet brought, the Hebraic characters were etched and shining. Kelner invited Don Moisés to express his opinion.

"The law," the distinguished visitor said, "obligates the judges to work for the reconciliation of the couple and so bring peace to the home. Therefore, my learned judges and prudent friends, I must stand by what I have said before."

Reb Joel and Reb Malaquías repeated their petitions. They cited the Talmud and the Books of Jurisprudence, the Bible and the best known judgments and commentaries. Finally the Shochet advised granting the divorce.

"Such is the will of God," Don Moisés asserted. "We met in accordance with the law and first refused the divorce, but then, listening to the clear reasoning of the couple's representatives in favor of the separation, and seeing that the man and wife cannot live together because there is no love between them, we have declared that this same law obligates us to grant the divorce—so that there may not be a Jewish home with such discord present; so that peace may be returned to the hearts of these two people! We have judged it in this way, and so we shall sign the grant, giving each of the two the right to remarry as honorable individuals."

Each of the judges signed the parchment, using his paternal but not his given name, in the manner prescribed for the synagogue. As he signed, Don Moisés congratulated the others and himself for the happy privilege they had as Jews. They found justice in their ancient codes as well as protection and security for individual liberty. He was moved—as a judge, as a Jew—and finished with this prayer: "Let us celebrate this judgment—in which so much of your discretion and wisdom shows—with wine! And let us praise God for having inspired us with justice and truth."

The wine was brought, and they touched glasses. Outside, the clear sunless sky was growing pale.

"It's the hour for prayer," Reb Malaquías said, "and there is a sufficient number of us to constitute a synagogue."

"Let our distinguished guest occupy the place of honor, the *umed*," said the Shochet, "and lead the prayer."

"This is a great honor, and I appreciate it," Don Moisés said. "Let us pray."

Don Moisés Urquijo de Albinoim lifted his arms towards the East and began with the words in praise of God, pronouncing them in the Spanish manner: "*Baruch attu Adonai* . . . Blessed are Thou, O Lord!"

> *Don Nuño de Guevara has stolen my sword and has said that this was done by Don Moisés de Sandobal, who is a Jew and, therefore, an enemy of God; and that he, Don Nuño, does not sin in not telling the truth because his father Confessor does consider it a great virtue and benefit to put the blame on Jewish dogs and not on decent Christians.*
> DON GUILLERMO RAIMUNDO DE MONCADA, COUNT
> OF MARMILA AND MASTER OF AITOTA, IN A LETTER
> TO DON FELIPE DE MONTRAL.

twenty two

THE CASE OF THE STOLEN HORSE

A few miles north of Karmel stands the sad little ranch of Don Brígido Cruz. His entire livestock has ample room in his corral, even though it is the small, circular type made of attached wooden posts. There is a gnarled, twisted post in the center, decorated with many pieces of skin left by the animals as they scratched their hides against the old tough wood.

It happened that someone stole a horse from Don Brígido, a lean, sorry nag with a filthy hide and a slow, weary walk. The Gaucho—known in the vicinity as "The Leaner"—never had saddled the nag, but used to rent her out to drag scrapers separating grain. Still, the horse had been stolen.

One day, the Leaner appeared in the colony in search of his horse. He met Jacobo in front of the butcher shop and spoke to him. "Tell me, little *gringo*," he said, "haven't you seen my trotter around?"

Jacobo hadn't seen any strange horse, but he asked for details and promised to help as much as he could by looking around. "neighbors must help each other, my friend," he said.

That same afternoon, on a trip to Balvanera, Jacobo looked and inquired for the horse, but he saw nothing and no one knew anything about it.

The following week, Don Brígido appeared again. He was sure, he said, that the horse had been stolen by Jews. He told this to the Shochet, in words that were delicately scented with the breath of alcohol.

Rabbi Abraham listened in silence, and then—as was customary for an old debater—meditated on what had been said. When he answered, his tone was courteous and persuasive, and he used gestures to help along his sparse Spanish vocabulary.

"Don Brígido, you're absolutely right in looking everywhere for your horse, and the Commissary should punish the one who's stolen it. But are you certain that it was stolen by someone in Rajíl?"

The Leaner looked at Don Abraham, twisted the reins on his saddle horn, and began to slowly roll himself a cigarette. As he finished, he looked at Don Abraham again with his small, unsteady eyes. "Now, look, *gringo*," he said. "I *know* that my horse has been stolen."

"That's absolutely right!" Rabbi Abraham said. "The horse is too old to have walked away by itself, and so, if it's gone, it must have been stolen by someone."

"Correct!" said Cruz.

Don Estanislao Benítez came up at that moment and cut the conversation short. The respect and obeisance due his fellow Argentine made Don Brígido contain himself. Briefly and courteously he told his story to Don Estanislao. Benítez calmed him and assured Brígido that he knew the Jewish colonists well and that, in his opinion, no one of them was capable of horse-stealing. Some local knave must have snatched it, Don Estanislao thought, and it was probably being hidden in the tall grasslands outside San Gregorio. A couple of his mares had once been stolen, and he had found them and the bandit there.

Don Brígido seemed convinced as he rode off. Don Estanislao said to his friend, Rabbi Abraham: "He's a brave one, that fellow, but he's very stubborn."

One morning, the Shochet was called to Villaguay, where the local functionary—who was a "good friend" of the Minister's—informed Rabbi Abraham that he had received a very strong denunciation of him. Don Brígido had accused Rabbi Abraham of having stolen his horse.

He wasn't surprised, Rabbi Abraham told himself. This wasn't a singular case by any means. The Gaucho, he thought, is not the same as a Russian *mujik*, but he himself is still the same Jew, and apparently the situation doesn't change. A horse is stolen? Then it must be a Jew who stole it. With Israelite skepticism—accustomed as he was to suffer for crime he had not committed and to pay the debts of others— Rabbi Abraham realized now that the tradition was working even here. He smiled at the Inspector and, taking a pinch of snuff, asked him: "My dear Sir, do you know of a code of law that isn't written down and that I like to think of as the code of law for decent men?"

"No, I don't know of it," the Inspector answered in a dry, stern voice. He was keeping his air of authority; it was doubly due him, as a functionary of police and as a "friend" of the Minister's. "I do not," he said.

"Well, Señor Jefe, it's like this," Rabbi Abraham plunged on. "The day before yesterday the overseer of the breakwater came and told me that my Gaucho helper, Facundo, had stolen a shovel from him. Now, Facundo doesn't need a shovel and besides, he's an honest boy. I sent the overseer away in quick time. That's what you ought to do with Don Brígido."

There was silence in the station for a long moment. The sergeant, whose face was scarred by honorable sword cuts and the mark of small-pox, continued to feed the fire under the inevitable *maté*, while the clerk who had been taking notes stared at his book.

Rabbi Abraham thought of something. "Don Brígido is asking fifteen pesos retribution, correct?"

"That's right, Don Abraham."

"Well, Señor Jefe," the Shochet went on, "I'm a very busy man these days. You tell me I'll have to come back Tuesday, and we're right in the middle of harvesting. I will give you the fifteen pesos and you can send them to Don Brígido, and then the thing will be finished."

The Inspector agreed, and the matter was closed. When Don Estanislao heard about it, he laughed and called Don Abraham a very wise man. He thought the matter had ended in the most convenient way for everyone.

On the other hand, the local functionary thought Rabbi Abraham something other than a wise man. From that day on, he used to say, "They're thieves, those Jews—but I'll say one thing for them. They confess right away."

It may be that Rabbi Abraham did not see the ultimate results of his act, but he did have a foreboding that the eternal condemnation of the Jews had somehow been transplanted to Argentina. Beneath his Solomon-like wisdom, he felt a strong prophetic pessimism.

Yes, it was still the Jew who had robbed anything in the neighborhood that was found missing, who was the instigator of any imaginable crime. And why? Because the Jew wore a long beard, because the Jew spoke respectfully to his Gaucho helpers and had them eat with him at his own table, rather than in the kitchen with the dog and the cats.

Will it always be like that? he thought. No! He believed—he did!—that the sons of his sons, living in the second century of the great Argentine Republic, would hear praise of Jewish deeds, would hear the praises sung after the Catholic *Te Deum* in the stately vastness of the Argentine cathedrals.

Oh, wait for those days, he cried, my find Jewish comrades of the colony! Patience, like suffering, is the ennobling gift and treasure of the sorry race of Job!

twenty three

REVOLUTION

In the old days, the post of Mayor was eagerly sought by the most re-spectable men in the colony. The post lent a certain prestige and au-thority, especially in regard to official functions when it was the Mayor who greeted the Argentine Administrator or the special envoy from the Jewish Committee. the colonist would all be present to welcome such dignitaries and they felt a vague kind of respect and envy for their Mayor as they watched him treat these famous people so famil-iarly and then take them to the official lunch or dinner.

"The Mayor" was a rather pompous title for the holder of the post because his duties were meager and mediocre. They consisted of pre-senting the very ordinary demands of the colonists to the Adminis-tration—such as a request for a new yoke, or for a new cow, because the present one could not be domesticated—or for a new horse, be-cause the present one had gone lame. In spite of this, the Mayor's work was characterized by the same passionate bias and quarreling that goes with any public office in any well organized society.

The Mayor was chosen—in strict accordance with the democratic procedure—by popular assembly. These meetings were always tumultuous, for even the most placid of the colonists would take a vocal part in the Jacobin oratory that featured an election.

In the time of which I write, Reb Isaac Stein was finishing his first term. Twenty-eight colonists formed a solid group of opposition to his re-election, but a number of others were still faithful to him. The situation was grave, and the comments in the synagogue skirted dangerously around the heart of the situation and foretold the coming blow-up.

One Saturday morning, in the patio of the rustic temple, the people were talking about the Mayor and some were using harsh words against humble little Stein.

Reb Israel Kelner was particularly aggressive, and Rabbi Abraham, a fair and sober man, agreed with him and stroked his long beautiful beard. Little Jacobo, always the best informed person in the colony, told of an incident concerning Stein that he thought was disgraceful.

"I was in the blacksmith shop of the Administration . . . ," he began.

Reb Israel, looking very solemn in his ritual tunic, put a fatherly hand on the boy's shoulder and said, "Boys shouldn't occupy themselves with politics. After all, Reb Isaac is a respectable old man."

Jacobo looked at Israel very sternly, tilted his gaucho hat and hitched at his belt that held a knife and *bolos*. "You're right, Reb Israel," he said with forced coldness. "But, remember this—if boys shouldn't concern themselves with such things, you mustn't ask me to vote for you."

Rabbi Abraham coughed discreetly and Kelner tried to smile. The boys and young men standing about waited expectantly; some were smiling, some were not. Finally, Kelner said: "you're always the same, Jacobo. You don't respect anything. As you were saying, then, you were in the blacksmith shop . . ."

"In the blacksmith shop of the Administration," Jacobo said. "I'd gone to find a grating. Reb Isaac was there—he wasn't Mayor at the time. After Isaac left, the blacksmith noticed that a roll of copper wire was rolling out. The end of it had been attached to something and the roll was slowly unwinding. The blacksmith caught on at once. He attached the other end of the wire to a post and called us all to watch. Isaac Stein was riding away at a slow trot on his little piebald. Suddenly the copper wire tautened and stretched like a tight guitar string, and then we saw Isaac's horse stop suddenly and Isaac bounce right over the head of the horse and on to the ground. He fell like a bale of goods.

"He got up slowly, detached the wire from the ring on his saddle girth. He looked at us and then remounted, and went on his way.

"That night he spoke to me about it, and said: 'Did you see what happened there, Jacobo? Did you ever see anything like that! I don't know who could have done a thing like that to me—attach that wire end to my saddle.'"

Some of the others told stories about the Mayor that were just as interesting, and the general conclusion was that the Mayor had humiliated the colony.

"I asked him to get a new yoke for me," one of the men said. "That was three months ago, and he still hasn't got one for me."

"And what about Rosilla?" another said. "He still hasn't gotten me a cow to replace her. She's a wild one—I can't milk her, whether I tie her down or have her held."

The complaints against Reb Isaac continued. Everyone had a similar charge of some failure against him. Meanwhile, from inside the synagogue the sound of fervent prayers was heard.

"Here comes the Mayor now," Jacobo said.

They saw Reb Isaac's very broad silhouette moving along the dusty road. When he came up to them, he was smiling broadly and greeted everybody affably: "Good Sabbath, Hebrews!"

"Good Sabbath, good year!" they answered.

The Mayor noted the cold attitudes in the answer. He thought the atmosphere was not too favorable to him, and decided to try to win the sympathy of his enemies. "It's a beautiful day, isn't it?" he said. "It's nice that it's a Sabbath today, because we can rest from the work of the week, and enjoy the excellent weather while the young folks enjoy themselves any way they please."

Israel Kelner, who prided himself on being a very fair person, said, "That's true."

The Mayor was encouraged. He launched into a wordy and amiable speech that included warm praise for each of his listeners. It was only yesterday afternoon, he said, that he was passing Guintler's field and noticed his wheat. "Magnificent!" he exclaimed. "Magnificent wheat!" He described the broad packed field fervently. "And Kelner's orchard! In what other colony, Reb Israel, can one see an orchard like yours? It cheers one just to look at it."

"I've worked hard on it," Kelner answered.

The Mayor did not forget to include the boy, Jacobo, in his praise. He patted him on the shoulder. "And that pony of yours, Jacobo! That's an animal that a prince would envy you. It's worth a lot of money. Do you know what? I'd even be willing to exchange my horse, my good horse, for that little pony."

"You'd be cheated," Jacobo said. "The pony's a little wild and you have to know how to handle him."

Stein was a little taken aback by the boy's cold answer. He felt it was time that he went in to pray, and put on his robe and entered the synagogue.

The elections were announced for next month. Kelner promised the Mayor's opposition that if he, Kelner, were elected, he would concern himself with serious matters, and work for the building of a school and a synagogue.

He made this promise in a speech at Guintler's house and went on to reproach Stein for his indifference and ingratitude. He was elected.

Immediately, his former friends and supporters found that he, too, had faults. Like Stein, he took his time replacing broken farm implements or adding to the livestock, and he was often proud, scornful and inattentive. Once, at the Administration office, the Shochet asked him to hasten the delivery of a replacement of his plow that had been broken when his ox team took fright and bounded off. It was sowing time and the new plow was badly needed, but Kelner had the audacity to tell the Shochet: "Let me alone. I'm very busy now."

The incident was commented on all over the colony, and created a good deal of displeasure. The women were particularly indignant at the insult to a man of the Shochet's prestige.

"Who would have thought it possible!" they said. "This deserves some punishment."

The Mayor's action crystallized the growing opposition to him, and Isaac Stein found himself at the head of the now forceful group. This was strictly in accordance with an ancient custom that always placed the recently deposed Mayor at the head of the opposition to the new Mayor, said opposition then being in the majority. Turbulent meetings were held, and at the last of these the first order of business was to find the quickest and surest way to depose Kelner.

But nothing was decided, and the controversy grew in heat and loquacity; at all hours in Rajíl, groups could be seen and heard discussing the Mayor. Then, one day, Kelner outdid himself when he forcibly ejected Isaac Stein from his house. The people's anger burst; a meeting to bring some action was called for that very night. Meanwhile, the younger folks went back to work in the fields and the old men went to the synagogue to meditate.

"How would it be if we went to see the Mayor?" Rabbi Abraham asked the other old men.

They discussed this risky possibility and then decided to do it. At the conclusion of their daily prayers, they started out for Kelner's house at the other end of the village.

There were eight of them. They moved slowly along the path in twos, and the breeze added to their dignity by gently blowing their long beards to and fro in the same quiet rhythm as their walk.

As they passed by the first houses, the women—who were at their daily chores with brooms and brushes—wanted to know the reason for the "procession." Where were they going, with such dignity? "To see the Mayor," one of the old men answered with no little coldness.

"Is that so?" First one woman, then two, then a third and more joined the procession. As it passed by other houses, other women fell in, still clutching a broom or brush, and shouting their ideas.

"We'll get the books from him!" one of them shouted.

"The books! Yes, the books!"

The "books" were actually a single notebook, provided by the Administration office, for the Mayor to list the requests and complaints of the colonists. It was the one visible symbol of his authority.

When he saw them coming, Kelner appeared at his doorway in great alarm. "What do you want?" he called out to them as the crowd came into his patio.

"We want the books!" a woman shouted.

"Yes, the books!" other women repeated. "The books!"

Kelner started a speech. He was a fluent speaker. This time, though, his words did not have their usual effect. He saw that the old men were being convinced, but the anger of the women grew as his voice became softer and more insinuating. Finally, his temper broke, and he shouted. "What am I doing, anyway? These are things that shouldn't even be discussed with women!"

"What's that?" a woman shouted back. "What are you saying, you monster?" Another woman threw her broom in his face. This was the signal for an uprising. The women rushed past Kelner and swarmed into the house, knocking down everything that stood in their path. They found the precious notebook.

It was Stein's wife who appeared at the big window, smiling triumphantly and holding the notebook up in her hand for the crowd to see.

The procession turned now and went back into the village, the notebook carried in front like a standard of victory, and the brooms and brushes being waved like banners.

And so ended the Revolution of Rajíl—a revolution that had so much in common with all the revolutions we read about.

> Let us honor—for his long and faithful service—the patriarch who rests beneath this stone, awaiting the Messiah and the resurrection. Rewarding his many years, God—do not say His name if you are not free of sin!—made a place for him in Paradise.
>
> INSCRIPTION IN ALJAMAIADO, ARABIC WRITTEN IN SPANISH CHARACTERS.

twenty four
THE OLD COLONIST

We always called him by his biblical name, Guedali. We could not remember his family name. It had probably been composed by a seventeenth-century "gentleman" who like to mock the Jewish rag dealers imprisoned in the sordid ghettos of Frankfurt or Munich. Guedali, we called him, or, better still, in the traditional manner, Reb Guedali ben Schlomo.

He certainly deserved to be addressed in that way, because, far from suggesting a colonist or farmer, he whole manner and bearing recalled the noble Jewish doctors, scientists and poets of medieval Spain. Only the Jews that Rabbi Menasche ben Israel writes of have such stature.

Guedali had a noble bearing and a quiet, majestic air. His face was always pale, as if from constant thinking, and his mouth ever smiling, in spite of the suffering he had known.

He was my teacher and it was he who taught me, in the rude comfort of his country house, the use of the ritual symbols and the meaning of our prayers. We venerate him justly, because he was truly venerable.

I knew him as an old man who went every morning and night to the synagogue. He looked like an old patriarch, walking slowly and thoughtfully, and leaning on his curved stick. He was old and wise, but he was tolerant too, as all men ought to be who have lived long in this world and have seen much. He was unable to work at this time, and he spent his days in bringing some touch of divine wisdom to the children. He taught them to appreciate God's gift of life and, at the same time, taught them the consolation they must give to the troubled hearts of the old and the dying.

He had the true bearing of the teacher and the saint. Age had thinned out his once solid and robust figure, and his calm measured walk gave him a simple, spiritual appearance. He seemed to be blessing you when he lifted his thin, trembling hand, and when he raised his eyes to God in prayer, his face lighted by his heart's feelings, he reminded one vividly of the old rabbis in our classic painting.

One day, towards evening, we saw him approaching our house, and, as he always did, he greeted us in Hebrew as he came up to the door:

"May God grant that I come to this house at a good time!"

Then, as soon as he had entered and caught his breath, he inhaled a full pinch of snuff that he picked from his antique box with its well-worn reproduction from the Old Testament on the cover. After he had highly praised our wheat and the cow that was quietly munching in the yard outside, Reb Guedali announced to my mother that he had come about a very important subject.

"Your son, Madam," he said, "is fatherless, and he must be taught the doctrines. As you know, orphans must be confirmed at the age of twelve. It will be a great pleasure to me to instruct him, so that he will know how to pray for his own, and how to give thanks to God."

From that day then, as soon as I had turned the animals into the pasture, I would go to Reb Guedali's house. In his mouth, the language of the prophets and the great rabbis recovered its primitive beauty, and after we had gone through the prayers he would explain the meaning of the psalms to me and the great value of Talmudic knowledge. In the way of the great Spanish and Arabic Hebraists, he would refer to the discussions of the ancient masters who had delved so deeply and subtly into the meanings of theology, ethics and morals. He could move easily through the confusing subtlety and depth of these works, and neither the Guemara nor the Cabala could hide any secret from Guedali's brave, probing mind.

One day, he said to me: "The man who has a well-developed mind but no kindness of heart is like someone who has only one eye on the side of his head and can see in only one direction. I'll tell you about a case, my son, that caused a good deal of discussion. This happened in Spain, when our people were living peacefully and happily under the Kings of Castile.

"Rabbi Akiva asked his pupils just what it was that a man needed in order to enjoy a full, happy life. One pupil said that he must have a faithful friend living near so that he could benefit by the friend's experience in life. Another said that he must have good health. A third said intelligence, and a fourth, wisdom.

"When Rabbi Akiva still said nothing, another pupil who had kept silent now spoke up. It would be necessary, he said, for a man to have all these qualities together—all these feelings and all this wisdom contained harmoniously in one man, in the same way that the colors of the rainbow are contained in the light of the sun. Such a man, he said, would never despair, though he be alone in the most solitary spot on earth.

"Do you see, my son?" Reb Guedali said to me. "And now, let us begin our prayers. We don't want the dinner hour to catch us feeling unworthy of God's blessings."

When his sons and grandsons were to cut the first furrows in their fields, it was Guedali who guided the plow. This was an important, solemn ceremony, and the old man gave it the same religious sense that the simple act of plowing receives in the land section of the Talmud. Guedali dressed himself in his ancient but thick greatcoat of furs, and, once the field had been marked and properly flagged, he held the handles of the plow and guided the curved knife as it cut into the earth behind the steady, earnest motion of the ox team. The first furrow done, he would sit on a rock and watch the young men work, calling out encouragement:

"Remember, Abraham, my son, remember, Jacob, my treasure—it may be difficult to earn one's bread from the soil, but that's the only way that honorable men earn it—work the land! I wish my hands had never touched any other thing but the Sacred Text and the plow. I would be certain to be in Paradise to watch over you then."

When he returned to the shepherd's hut nearby, where his wife sat waiting for him and warming her old body the *brasero*, he said to her: "I left our children at the field. They know how to honor us with hard work. God give us a good year, and may those poorer than we have one, too! Have you prayed and eaten yet?"

On the day I was confirmed, the neighbors came to my house to congratulate me and, as customary, they ate sweet bread and drank wine. That afternoon I heard Reb Guedali tell the story of his life.

The old man, whose life was now so filled with religion and precepts, had once been the founder of a city. As a very young man in Russia, he found himself the owner of a huge fortune in land and wealth. Feudalism was still existent in Russia and the large landowners were actual masters of the slave serfs. It was the time, too, in Russia when the Czar's soldiers would make excursions into the Polish province, capture some rich landlord, hang him and then, according to the stories, sell his clothes and jewels to wandering Austrian peddlers.

When Reb Guedali acquired his land, he began to turn most of the produce over to his tenants who had worked the land. In the eyes of the Imperial officers, this marked him at once as an enemy of the state and a threat to law and order. Guedali was warned, but would not conform—nor would he wait for some drunken troops to come and hang him. He journeyed to St. Petersburg to put his case before the Czar, carrying an antique Pentateuch and a beautiful string of pearls as gifts for the ruler.

"Here is a good Jew," said Nicholas I. "We must respect him." He granted Guedali special privileges on his lands.

Shortly after that, feudalism was abolished, and Guedali was deprived of all his land. His fortunes suffered even more serious losses during the war undertaken by Czar Alexander II. He was still rich, however, and continued to live in the city he had established until he heard of the colonies in America. He had journeyed to Jerusalem before, but had returned saddened, and declared that he preferred to live in any place but the crowded square that was the sacred capital of the Jews, with its convents, its crosses and its minarets. He came to Entre Rios with the first immigrants. Here, he had realized his ideal; to work the land, to eat bread made from his own wheat and beans grown in his own garden.

One morning, a boy came to the house to say that Reb Guedali was asking for us. As we rushed to his house, we felt the fear that his last hour had come, and when we came to his place, already crowded with people, we found him seated in the center of the big room, dressed in his white gown, still imposing, still serene. His life was flickering out, like a slowly dying lamp.

He said goodbye to each of us—with words of hope and gratitude—and then—lifting his eyes, he said to us all: "God grant that your bodies, like mine, may rest in this earth that you work with your own hands! Then we shall all be blessed . . ."

His voice lowered into silence, and his eyes closed as the sobs of his people grew louder.

That was the way my teacher lived; that was the way he died.

twenty five
THE MIRACULOUS DOCTOR

The girls of Rajíl, Rosch Pina, Espíndola and San Gregorio, and the widow with hazel eyes who lived on the outskirts of Karmel, were surprised and upset to learn that a new doctor had taken over the practice of the colonies.

"Will he be like Doctor Richene?" the widow asked, as she smoothed her hair with one hand and with the other adjusted the well-worn, braided moiré sash whose chief purpose, it seemed, was to draw attention to her fine thin waist. "Will he?"

The question reflected the deep and lasting place that Doctor Richene held in the memory of all the colon's women. When they knew he would be in the neighborhood, they used to stand in their doorways, dressed as if for a holiday, and watch him go by on his sorrel-colored horse with its English saddle. His beard would be waxed, his sun helmet worn at a jaunty angle, his trousers held with a belt of fine skin, and his boots well shined.

No! It would be difficult for this new doctor to resemble *the* Richene who had one sweetheart to every five farms and two more in each of the three railroad junctions, not counting the girl in Colón whose house had balconies with bronze railings. But would he at least be something like the doctor's assistant at the hospital in Domínguez—that giant of a man, with shoulders like bundles of corn in a good year, who brought sweets to his patients, was brusque in his examinations, and sometimes patted the wrong spot as he talked soothingly to his female patients?

My cousin Jantze said of the new doctor: "I'm sure he must be single."

"He's sure to be married," said Eva, who lived on the other side of the bridge and who every spring seemed doomed to break the betrothal she had worked so hard to make in the fall. That was the harvest time and many young men came from outside to work at the threshers.

"They tell me," Oxman's wife said, "that his wife lives in Paris."

"In Paris?" said the widow. "Paris?" She sighed deeply and sadly. "She must have her photograph taken often."

In person, Nahum Yarcho disillusioned the girls and disappointed the widow. In place of a sun helmet, he wore a slouch hat that was always falling off his head as he got up into his sulky, and, in place of patent leather boots, he wore canvas shoes with yellow skin tips. The pride he took in these outrageous shoes was scandalous to the women.

He was professional, at least, in his use of eyeglasses—they were gold-rimmed, naturally, and were always misted and lopsidedly set on the bridge of his long, thin, curved nose—for it must be admitted that Doctor Yarcho was not a pure Aryan, as we speak of it today. On the contrary, in spite of having studied first in Russia and then in Paris and having read Tolstoi, he could always be seen making his way toward the shelter in the synagogue on Saturday mornings, a diminutive figure, with, of course, that same slouch hat and those same outrageous shoes. This does not mean that he paid strict attention to the service or denied himself his usual cigarette in the sacred province of Jehovah. Nahum Yarcho was something of an epicure, and so broke the rules with a smiling nonchalance.

Someone might ask, what was he doing, then, in the synagogue— particularly during those times when old Rubinstein lifted his voice in the rhythmic cadences of the prayers or when the chapters of the Pentateuch were being read in silent enjoyment? He was doing what he did for most of his simple and memorable life: telling stories, lis- tening to stories. He was one of those rare men we read about in nov- els of sorcery or in the lives of poets.

He delighted in talking to the old ladies, wrinkled and bent as they were, because their talk, so full of "Oh, my!" and "God help us!" still told him the juiciest secrets of the colonies. He liked talking to the old men even more—in spite of their inability to differentiate be- tween any two letters of the Hebrew script, they would readily dis- course with all the sophistry of a Talmudic scholar, voicing their well-rounded, well-chosen words with a serious mien that was spiced with malice, a malice as quick as a wink, as subtle and effective as the strong pinch of snuff they held between their fingertips. Those fingertips were brown now—from nicotine, time, and a frequent kneading of the phylacteries.

The first weeks of his practice were not very favorable for Yarcho. The hospital pharmacist, for one, was very displeased and made no bones about it. Doctor Yarcho was not prescribing salves or syrups, neither the red of green colored syrup in the more expensive frosted bottle or in the cheaper plain glass bottle. No, he was decidedly not prescribing medicaments in spite of the fact that he received so much advertising literature and was a subscriber to many French medical magazines.

And the Shochet's wife was quite put out by her first visit to the doctor in Domínguez. First of all her trip there was a veritable expedition—because the Shochet's wagon had a wheel off and in her impatience to get to the doctor's she decided to make the trip in the ox cart. The oxen were a servile and gentle pair, but they dragged the cart slowly and laboriously. They were highly prized for their obedience, answering commands in Yiddish and being equally aware of directions in the native Argentine, but they always obeyed slowly and sleepily, and as they trudged the slow two leagues to Domínguez their mouths did not miss a single blade of grass or wheat that bent in towards the road.

The doctor received her with pleasure. "I was expecting you, Madam," he said.

The Shochet's wife was deeply moved. Here, she told herself, was a wise doctor. He knew when his patients were coming, even though they were unannounced. Of course, she told herself further, he wouldn't bother to guess at the arrival of Jaimovich's wife—that common woman who dared to cook on the Sabbath, who pinched the young men at the wedding feasts, and who wore her corset so tightly that it was a disgrace! Oh, no! He would expect and wait for *her*, a first cousin to the Rabbi of Rosch Pina, a dutiful and virtuous woman—so amenable and compliant that she had born her last child on the exact date of her silver wedding anniversary.

"Were you waiting for me, truly?" she asked, after recovering from her surprise and having finally caught her breath.

"I was waiting for you, yes," continued the doctor. "Up to noon, I wait for the girls. They haven't got much to do, so they come to consult me before taking a turn through the stores to look over the laces and things."

"It's true, doctor. The girls of today are bird-brains. Take the wife of Jaimovich, for example. Now, she . . ."

"And in the afternoon," Yarcho went on, "I wait for the more serious ladies, who come to see me, tell me about their ailments, and then take a turn through the stores to look over the laces and things. You, on the other hand, aren't like that. No! You really ought to take care of yourself."

"My God, doctor! Am I that sick?"

"That sick, no. But still, you ought to take care of yourself. Everyone should take of oneself."

"Doctor Richene forbade me to eat meat."

Yarcho led her over to the window. The immense stretches of the plains were burning beneath the sun and the light itself seemed warm and alive in the diaphanous air. "Open your eyes wide," he said. "Do you see those clouds skimming along back there? They look like rosy little lambs. Did you ever see clouds like that in your terrible little village in Russia?"

"I don't usually look at clouds. I've got too much to do."

"Madam, you must look at clouds. Believe me, it's very good for the health."

"And what do you prescribe for me, doctor?"

"I advise you to eat a bit of meat, not to torment yourself too much, and not to take any medicines. Medicines hurt some people more than they help them. What's your favorite dish? Stuffed fish? Or maybe it's potato balls with roast beef? If I'm ever in your neighborhood, don't forget to invite me to eat. Oh, yes—in regard to your leg—don't pay any attention to it."

"How do you know my leg hurts?"

"Well, what did the good God give us legs for, if not to hurt? Do you want proof of that? Look at Don Isaac, the one from San Miguel. He never complains about his legs because he was born without them. I ask you, isn't it much better—so much better—for one's legs to hurt, as they do you, than for them not to hurt, as happens to Don Isaac?"

"It's incredible," the Shochet's wife was telling her neighbors later. "He didn't even give me a salve. Can he really be a doctor? But then," she said, as if she were confessing it to herself, and as if this might be a sin, "the curious things is that while he talks to you, one is smiling all the time. And the doctor himself smiles. And the strangest thing is that one forgets he's a doctor. He smiles and smiles. How he smiles!"

The folks of Rajíl, Rosch Pina, Espíndola and San Gregorio were living in a state of fearful waiting. It was not because of a drought or the current talk of revolution that had been motivated by the presence in Villaguay of a colonel from the capital of the province. Nor was it due to predictions of a new plague of locusts. No, the fear and expectancy was due to the dramatic discovery that Doña Maria, the hunchback, was expecting a child. The year before she had been expecting too, and Doctor Richene had become very alarmed when his examination seemed to confirm this.

"Your wife cannot bear a child," he told her husband.

Fortunately, the diagnosis was premature. In those days, Doña Maria was as far from bearing a child as she was close to it now—always providing that God's luck favored her and that the entire population was correct in its diagnosis. More than ever, her appearance now caused grief and worry, for Maria was in fact a little monster—despite her perfect face, her sad, glowing eyes under long dark eyelashes, her low timid voice that seemed to ask pardon for intruding into this world that was featured by women like Karmel's widow. She inspired grief and worry because that perfect face tottered unsteadily over a body that was distorted, that was little, that was miserable.

"Oh, my God!" she would moan. "What if my child should resemble me!"

"If it resembles you," Doctor Yarcho told her, "it will have your eyes, it will have your voice, and it will like to sing just as much as you do! Promise not to tell and I'll let you in on a little secret? God was a fellow student of mine at the University in Paris, and I assure you He always knows what He's doing. I know Him quite well."

The hunchback would smile at this—with her eyes, and with her hands, that were as pale and translucent as if they were already tenderly moved about the head of a child held to her breast.

"María will scream a lot, won't she, Doctor?" Señora Mirner asked Yarcho. By virtue of having helped with so many nephews, nieces and grandchildren, Señora Mirner had gradually taken over the position of colony midwife and assisted at all the births. "She will, won't she?" she said.

"Well, haven't you heard a lot of screaming in your time?" Yarcho asked. "What does it matter, really? You get a little sleep between screams, don't you? Tell me, what have you heard of the Benjamin Riber divorce?

"The same as everybody else! I'm not deaf, you know. I can't help hearing about that. And I don't like to repeat gossip, of course, but I think that Riber's an unfortunate wretch. Imagine!—during Passover, his wife went to the temple with rouge on her cheeks!"

Then, one Sunday at dusk, the doctor's sulky was seen standing in the hunchback's yard. (She was called the "hunchback," not because of a hump on her back, but because that was the only physical disfigurement that she lacked.) María lay quietly stretched on the bed, her eyes absorbed in thought, but she began to smile as soon as the little doctor had come up to the head of her bed and smiled down at her. Her terror began to fade then; her fear began to move away.

"What a beautiful room you have, María!" Yarcho said as he looked around. "Your room seems to sing—just as you do. It looks like, María—happy and expectant. Soon it will have a son, just as you will."

Outside in the broad street, shaded with paradise trees, the people of Rajíl waited anxiously and walked cautiously about.

The birds, too, seemed disturbed, and flew chattering from tree to tree. Squatting along the sharp edge of María's roof, the black cat meowed piteously, and her dog jumped about in the yard and barked at the moon. It was a bright round moon that seemed to seek everyone out, and was frightening the girls who were kissing their young men behind the harvesting machines. Doctor Yarcho came out to smoke a cigarette. The women rushed up to him.

"How strange, Doctor! She's not screaming."

"How can she? With such a beautiful moon! It would be disgraceful."

Jacobo, who was only fifteen but who already had some reputation as a rascal, a wonderful horseman and a great breaker of wild colts, looked up at the moon and tried to win Yarcho's attention with a question on astronomy. "What's the moon made of, Doctor?" he said.

"Glycerin and hard-boiled eggs."

"Does the moon ever fall?"

"It falls into the Parana every morning and, just before the stars come out at night, the Fisherman upstairs picks it out and rolls it into the sky. If you want to see it fall, climb up the big eucalyptus at Balvanera some night and stay there until dawn."

An owl hooted somberly in the darkness; a bat flew by and the dog's answering bark cut the silence. There was a cry from the room at their backs, stifled at first, but then loud and unashamed and growing.

The doctor was seen no more. As the door closed after him, they could see the bright metal of the heating pans inside shining in the light of the lamp.

After that night, Doctor Yarcho was spoken of with deep and religious respect. They spoke of his miraculous cures; they repeated his rare sayings. What was the source of these marvelous things in him? Where had the miracle started? they asked themselves. No one could explain it; no one doubted it. From the most humble, in the misty little settlements of Jewish colonists, to the rich and traditional families in the large cities of the province—everyone became more and more aware of his fame and reputation. He was called from the farthest outskirts of the province and the doctor of Gualeguay used to journey into the hospital at Domínguez to consult with him about his most complicated cases. Doctor Pita—of the Córdoba Pitas!—advised him one day. "My dear Yarcho, you're missing all your chances sticking to these little villages. Go to Buenos Aires; you'll get rich and famous there!"

"More famous than here? That won't be easy," Yarcho said. "Everybody bows to me here, and everybody always helps me fix the reins of my sulky. I don't know what they use to make those reins in Crespi—mine break on an average of once a day. And as far as being rich, I think I am. I've got twenty-three hectares of land, two pairs of shoes, and my wife just came back from Uruguay with a new hat."

"Don't joke, Yarcho. It's a shame that you won't go to Buenos Aires, but, at least, go to Parana. They'll make you a Deputy in a year there."

"Really? I'm glad you told me that. I was thinking of visiting Parana next week, but after hearing that I don't think I'd want to go. And I thought the Governor was a friend of mine! Trust to the politicians!"

"Oh, you're always joking. You joke about everything."

"No, I don't, my friend. I live very seriously. What would I do in Buenos Aires? What would I do in Paraná? In Buenos Aires and in Paraná people suffer, they get tired, get full of despair, feel pains they imagine and don't seem to feel pains that are killing them—just as the people in Villaguay do, and in Domínguez, in Rajíl, and in Las Moscas. Here, in the mornings, in my garden, with a book on my knees, I can pass hours sitting under the paradise tree where the larks nest—that is, if my patients let me. I'm on very familiar terms with the larks, and none of your big city doctors can have that. Don't bees delight you, by the way?"

Pita stared at him. "That must be why Macia says you're a philosopher," he said, after a moment. "That, and because of the story of the little drink."

The story of "the little drink" was a very famous one. A rancher from La Capilla came to consult Doctor Yarcho privately about his son's drinking.

"I'm very worried, Doctor. Very worried! I don't know where he inherits it from. Imagine! I'm over fifty and I've never touched a drop of alcohol."

Yarcho jumped up suddenly. "Guterman!" he called, going into the hall. "Bring that bottle of sherry. Right away!" He turned to the astonished rancher. "You're not leaving without trying a drink."

"But, do you drink?" the rancher asked. "You?"

"I drink, eat and sleep, and ride around in a sulky."

"I can't believe it."

"Furthermore, my religion demands it," the doctor said. "The ritual that forbids me to eat unclean meat demands that I bless wine. Since I don't know the blessings from memory, I comply with the law by drinking the wine."

"That's all right, but if one drinks to excess . . ."

"I can't drink to excess, because I haven't got time to be thirsty. On the other hand, I know we have to be careful about excesses. Do you remember what happened to Israel Fajman? That poor man? He was so devout, and he was so willing. From the moment he got up until he went to bed, he would do nothing but pray. One time, while he was praying, his ranch burned down. Since that day, he's never prayed again. How do you like that sherry? It's a present."

"From the Governor?"

"No, the priest at Concordia gave it to me."

The Treasurer of Villaguay added considerably to his own growing reputation as a philosopher by virtue of the many Yarcho stories he told. In his simple, picturesque language he would entertain the farmers on his rounds with stories of Yarcho's attempts to navigate his sulky through the mired, muddy country around Vergara. Philosopher or not, however, the Treasurer could understand very little of the speech Yarcho made to a neighborhood meeting called for the purpose of discussing municipal improvements in Villaguay.

"It's very simple," the doctor said, "to fix up our plaza, our churches, in fact, our whole little city. Last Tuesday, I was coming up from Domínguez and my little horse was so wrecked with fatigue that I stopped to rest him. I was just sitting there, staring out in front of me when I saw a city—about two kilometers away. It was a brightly lit and shining city, with golden towers, golden cupolas, golden palaces, and golden trees. I'll bet, I said to myself, that the doctor in that city has a golden sulky.

"Well, I started to move off then, and I kept thinking: wouldn't it be possible to build an exact copy of that city that was moving in front of me on the horizon? I think it's stupid to copy ugly things. If I were ever elected Treasurer, I'd just take that city I saw in the clouds there and build it up around the four sides of our plaza."

The Gauchos would never hesitate to call him at midnight or at dawn. Doctor Yarcho would sleepily lope along in his unsteady sulky for a dozen leagues or more to save a child from diphtheria, to operate on a wound, or to assist some disinherited soul that the polite doctors would not deign to visit. He would even go to those grassy regions around San Gregorio that served as hideouts for the cattle rustlers or some careless knife wielder seeking cover from the Vazquez police. In the cane or tin shacks, there Yarcho would open his valise and distribute the needed drugs freely so that none of the fugitives would have to risk a trip into town and a possible meeting with the police.

Once, on his way to San Salvador, he suddenly came upon a group of rustlers who were driving some calves they'd just stolen from the Escrina herd. It was pouring and thundering—the night sky seemed to have burst its seams—and one of the startled rustlers quickly grabbed the reins of the doctor's team and pointed his gun at the sulky. A sudden flash of lightning lit up the man's face.

"González!" the doctor shouted from his seat. "How's that arm of yours? Has the break completely healed?"

"It's the doctor!" González and his friends recognized whom they had stopped. "The doctor!" they said. "Yes. It's him!"

"Since you're right there, González," Yarcho was saying now, "fix that right rein for me, will you?"

And so, the Jews of the synagogue, the Gauchos of the plains, and the women of the colonies all hailed his wonderful skill, his kindly genius, his stories and his infectious smile. The women felt a new tenderness towards him, and even Karmel's widow had forgotten about the incomparable Doctor Richene.

"My God, that smile!" she exclaimed, feeling an inner agitation that showed only slightly in her blushes.

"And how he talks!" Aída said—the same Aída who had barely missed complete disgrace and ostracism because of that business with the young man from Benítez. At the time of that happening—something that nobody mentioned but that nobody forgot—Aída's mother sought out Doctor Yarcho for advice.

"I'm disgraced, Doctor. Completely disgraced," she said. "My daughter . . ."

"Your daughter is the prettiest girl around here," Yarcho said. "A magnificent girl, Madam."

"Yes, but instead of getting married, like any decent girl . . . Oh, I'm so disgraced, Doctor! So disgraced!"

"What do you mean, instead of getting married? She's married! She was married in Diamante. I was a witness at her wedding. Sandoval and I! You know Sandoval, don't you? Gregorio Sandoval. Of course, you do!"

After the pleased and reconciled mother had left, Yarcho called in Guterman. "Now, don't forget," he warned him. "Sandoval and I were witnesses at the wedding ceremony. By luck, the poor devil of a boy who caused all the trouble died in Uruguay, and he won't be able to make liars of us. Neither will Sandoval—because we don't know any Sandoval."

Years and years later, they would still remember Yarcho. Talking over his life, a rabbi would say: "He was a saint. I never knew a Jew who was more honorably Jewish."

The Commissary would scratch at the scar on his cheek and say, "He was a true Gaucho."

The women—the poor women, the beautiful women—who understand the facts of life better than the Rabbi or Commissary—the women would sigh: "Oh, when he smiled! When he used to smile in that way of his!" And the women—the poor women, the beautiful women—would smile softly, remembering . . .

twenty six

THE SILVER CANDELABRA

Today the farm was bathed in a deep, clear dawn of autumn sunlight whose warmth seeped around the thick wall of the adobe house. From its little open window, the country could be seen stretching lazily towards the far hills of yellowing thistle and a solitary paradise tree. Close to the house, the cow nestled at a rope's length and licked at the buttocks of her young calf.

It was Saturday, and the little house shared the colony's quiet. An occasional hum of a neighbor's song or prayer were the only sounds heard. Guedali had put on his white tunic and was quietly voicing the first prayers when his wife came in. He noticed her and made a sign to her not to interrupt him. He nodded towards the door.

The wife stood looking about for a moment, then turned and went out as quietly as she had come in. Guedali heard her talking to their daughter on the other side of the doorway. "I couldn't ask him," she was saying. "He's already begun his prayers."

Guedali was very religious. He was not ranked among the most learned men of the colony, and he rarely distinguished himself at the synagogue when some obscure point of the texts or commentaries was being discussed. Still, he was very religious.

He was a mild-mannered man, with a soft, serious voice. His deeply set eyes were shadowed by full, graying brows, but a sweet, timid look always showed in his eyes, like a flame that gave no heat. Guedali looked taller and thinner than ever as he faced the East and prayed now. The long tunic, reaching to the floor in full, uneven folds, appeared to elongate his thin, narrow frame.

He was very absorbed in his prayers when he suddenly felt someone outside moving towards his little window. He did not stop praying, but slowly turned his head to see who this was. It might be his neighbor, he thought, the one who had done his military service in the big city and who was always making fun of Guedali's devoutness. That one again! he thought.

It was not his neighbor he saw at the window, but an unknown man who was reaching in towards the candelabra—the silver candelabra that was the single inheritance from Guedali's noble past, a piece that enriched this poor little ranchhouse and that testified to the rich traditions of the presently poor colonists. The candelabra stood straight and majestic, glittering and pure, with its seven arched branches reflecting the sunlight so that the empty cups seemed to contain hidden ritual lights.

Guedali did not interrupt his prayer. He shot a stern look at the unknown man, and hissed out between the sacred phrases: "No! No! It's the Sabbath! It's the Sabbath!"

It was all he felt he could say without profaning his religious mood. "It's the Sabbath!" But the unknown man merely glanced at him, reached in and grabbed the candelabra, and quickly disappeared. Guedali continued praying, moving his shoulders in rhythm to the phrases of the verses. As he murmured the blessings, his voice had a sad, mournful tone, but he continued until he had finished the last prayer. Then he sighed deeply. The growing sunlight shone on his languid face with its wrinkled forehead and long sparse beard, growing whiter every day.

Guedali folded his tunic carefully and replaced it in the drawer of the sideboard. When his wife came in, he said very calmly, "They've stolen our candelabra." Guedali took a piece of bread from the table and began to eat.

His wife had stopped and was staring at him. "But . . . But . . ." she began. "Weren't you here?" she shouted indignantly. "Weren't you here? You piece of . . ."

Very calmly—like anyone convinced he has done his duty—Guedali answered her: "I told him that it was the Sabbath. I told him that," he said.